YES, A BIG ~~~~
OF YOUR FIELD,
BUT I HOPE IT'S
AN INTERESTING
READ, DR. FISH.

Rbld W F

7·28·2021

GOT AN INTERESTING
READ, OR. FISH.

Todd W.J.

7-28-2021

The Galilee Episode

Two Men in One Bed,
Two Women Grinding

RONALD W. GOETZ

BLOSSOM VALLEY TRUMPET
EL CAJON, CALIFORNIA

Blossom Valley Trumpet

whytestonne@hotmail.com

ISBN-13: 978-1-7338617-0-0
Published November 21, 2019

Front cover design by Hazel Huntsman.
Original cover art, "Castor and Pollux," by Rick Treat.
Book Design by Toby Johnson.

Library of Congress Cataloging-in-Publication Data

Goetz, Ronald W.
The Galilee Episode: Two Men in One Bed, Two Women Grinding
p. cm.
ISBN-978-1-7338617-0-0

1. Bible—Gay interpretations—Luke interpretation—Translation, 2. Persecution—History—Early church, ca. 30-600, 3. Judaism—History—To 70 A.D., 4. Yoḥanan ben Zakkai, d. ca. 80, 5. Law enforcement—History—Vice control, 6. Conspiracy theories. I. Goetz, Ronald W. II. Title.

Library of Congress Control Number: 2019903317

Contents

Acknowledgments

I want to acknowledge my first wife, Diane. She was with me when I began this research, and supported me warmly and tolerantly. She said, "There's no idea so sacred that Ron won't pick it apart and analyze it." She's passed now, but I owe her so much.

Lissette, Melanie, you have taught me a lot. I've watched you grow into adult women, which is one helluva challenge. And Jonathan, years ago you said, "Dad, you have to finish this book." If it weren't for you, I would never have even discovered all this.

Andy Welch, dear friend, thank you for listening to me go on and on about Luke 17, Yoḥanan b. Zakkai and all the rest. You poor guy! For your encouragement, for reading draft pages, for your valuable input, and for telling me my ideas deserved a public hearing, thank you.

Toby Johnson, Daniel Helminiak, Rocky Roggio—thank you for your invaluable contributions to *The Galilee Episode*. You helped me focus on what's really important.

My thanks to a professor whom I shall not name. So long ago, in a time of crisis, you were a help. I was on the edge. That afternoon you told me, "Don't stop writing."

Finally, Nital, my professor and poet, *Shucran Zojti, shucran ala kulshi.*

I want to mention some of the academics whose work enriched my understanding. I include John Kloppenborg and Burton Mack, Richard Horsley and William Arnal, Beth Berkowitz and Elias Bickerman, Sandra Gambetti and Samar Habib, Migaku Sato and Douglas Oakman. My greatest research debt is to Rabbi and Professor Jacob Neusner. In the early stages, my thesis was sharpened by readers at *Bible-Thumping Liberal*, and by several months of debate with the good people at *Sermon Index*.

Introduction

When I was a fundamentalist, they said, "Let the Bible say what it says. Don't force it to say what you *want* it to say." About twelve years ago I was researching the Clobber Passages when I read an anonymous blog comment: "I wonder why the homos haven't picked up on Luke 17:34 in the KJV." Intrigued, I opened my King James Bible. I had read this verse, heard it preached, but I was quite surprised. "I tell you, in that night, there shall be two men in one bed; the one shall be taken, and the other shall be left." In the following months and years I studied and investigated. In 2011 I first blogged about the gays and lesbians in Luke 17.

I began my research with a question, "Could Jesus have been talking about gay men in verse 34?" I had long since debunked the Clobber Passages after careful study, but I was not convinced that Jesus referred to gays and lesbians in Luke 17. I only knew that he *could* be. I looked at the immediate context. I looked up Old Testament antecedents. I studied word meanings. I knew that if a thesis as controversial as this was going to be taken seriously, that Jesus talked about gays and lesbians and was not condemning, it would need to be more than a Bible study comment like, "Well, gee, I think it means..." I had graduated from a Bible college, attended two Baptist seminaries, and read a lot in Bible and theology. I knew the difference between exegesis and opinion.

Months of research and every test was positive. I shared my amazement with my wife Diane. "Every time I ask a question, the answer is in plain sight, scattered on the ground like treasure. I can't believe I'm the first person to see this!" But when I did net searches combining *Luke 17:34-35* with keywords such as *homosexual* or *gay* or *lesbian*, I found nothing. If anyone had seen this recently, they weren't publishing, and apparently never had.

After I began posting about it in 2011 on my *Bible Thumping Liberal* blog, someone asked why, in two thousand years, no one had seen the gays and lesbians in Luke 17. I had puzzled over that question myself. Eventually I realized that the question was not correct. Many people *had* seen them, or at least seen the *possibility* that Jesus mentioned gays and lesbians in Luke 17. They saw how the verses could be interpreted that way, but they just *knew* that Jesus couldn't be talking about *them*. As a young person I'd heard many sermons on the rapture, and there was always a disavowal of any sexual content in the passage. "Just because they're in a bed doesn't mean anything *bad* was going on. I slept in the same bed with my brothers and sisters, and there was nothing sexual going on." I had experienced the same thing myself. My three siblings and I shared a hide-a-bed for a while and, it's true, nothing sexual was going on.

But my dispensational church taught that you weren't supposed to interpret the Bible based on your personal experience. The main application of that rule was different, of course. Some people, according to my church, erroneously equated the Baptism of the Holy Spirit with the gift of tongues. I heard that prohibition against interpreting the Bible to fit your experience quite often. Part of the problem: they didn't realize they were doing it themselves.

After months of investigating the possibility that Jesus was talking about gays and lesbians in Luke 17:34-35, it was confirmed time and time again, yet I still found no discussions of sexual orientation and Luke 17. Then I remembered that older churchmen used roman numerals in their scripture citations. Instead of looking for "Luke 17:34" I entered "Luke xvii: 34." Using the older citation style I found denials and explanations in English going back 300 years. One source was written before the American

Declaration of Independence. The explanations never directly refuted the presence of gays and lesbians. They specified where and what the action was.

There's no telling what discussions might be found in Latin, Russian, Greek, French, Slavonic or German. But in English I found that a number of churchmen bristled at the implication of two men in one bed.

But the question someone asked me is still valid. Why virtually nothing until now? People had seen the *prima facie* evidence of sexual activity in Luke 17: 34-35 but they only wrote about it to refute it. Apparently no one had sought out the kind of evidence necessary to mount a sustained argument supporting the gay and lesbian identity of the couples in Luke. Why now, at the beginning of the twenty-first century in North America, is the sexual orientation of the same-sex couples and their legal *sitz-im-leben* finally discernible? After all, the evidence has been available to us for a very long time. The sources have been there (the gospel of Luke, the Talmud, and Josephus) but access has been effectively restricted to a narrow segment of the population, the kind of people encouraged to study the classics, ancient history, the Bible, Talmud. Some people have called this wider access *democratization*, others have called it *diversity*. That last one is a bit amusing, me being a WASP and all.

Using the King James Version

Some have quibbled with my use of the King James Version, and with good reason. The earliest texts available to King James' translation team were from the tenth century. Today we have the Vaticanus (c. 300-325), Sinaiticus (c. 330–360), and Alexandrinus (400-440), codices and gospel fragments which date from the second century. Beyond the archaic "thees and thous," the evolution of the English language itself is a problem. Today the word *prove* means "to establish something," while in 1611 the idea of "testing" was dominant. Some word shifts are even more radical. The word *let* now means "to allow," in 1611 it meant "to prevent," the exact opposite (Rom. 1:13).

Beside the evolution of language is the problem of deliberate stylistic obfuscation, such as the KJV's use of the archaic word *concupiscence* in Colossians 3:5. Translated elsewhere as *lust*, the word *concupiscence* was already an artificial Latinism in 1611.[1] For Christians who value egalitarian intelligibility, the realization that some translators would choose to deliberately obfuscate the Bible seems quite incredible.

In the case of the KJV, some problems don't regard translation, but pertain to the actual texts. Fraudulent additions to the manuscripts vary in quality and severity. Some additions have been relatively harmless, such as the complicated addition of Luke 17:36. Certainly the most edifying of such fabrications happens to be many people's favorite passage, the *Pericope Adulterae* (John 7:53—8:11). The famous Woman taken in Adultery is, as wise men have said, the only gospel story to make it into the canon on merit.[2] On this note, objective scholars date the "discovery" of the book of the Law (Deuteronomy) to 622 BCE, in connection with the reforms of King Josiah. The official story of the book's advent is recounted in II Kings 22. Subsequently, Deuteronomy was famously described in 1807 by Wilhelm M.L. DeWette as a "pious fraud." Regarding the King James Version, the most egregious addition to find its way in is probably the notorious *Johannine Comma*, an explicitly trinitarian passage inserted into I John 5:7-8.[3]

I understand the increasing disuse of the King James Version, being simultaneously difficult, elegant, unreliable and even obfuscatory. I understand and concur. First, you're learning about Ultimate Reality. Second, you're adapting to a strange church culture. And you're going to add the further challenge of reading a

Bible written in Shakespearean English? Who reads Shakespeare without footnotes? Nevertheless, use the KJV text of Luke 17:34-35 for clarity and simplicity. There are no archaic words, no *thees* or *thou shalts*. There is, however, evidence of ideological tampering, recently added ideological tampering.

About forty-five years ago (around 1975), I took a Hebrew class at Simpson College from Richard O. Rigsby, who later became professor of Old Testament at Talbot Seminary. One day he told the seminar about a puzzle he'd been working on. "In the Genesis creation account, the tense of the verb changes between perfect and imperfect, and I can't figure out why. I've asked other Hebrew scholars about it, and they don't know either." A week or two later a student, Daphne Downard, had an explanation. She said it related to the nature of the act, to complete and incomplete action. I don't remember the specifics, but Professor Rigsby was impressed. He later told us of how he had shared Daphne's discovery with a colleague who replied, "Well, of course." I learned early there were still discoveries to be made.

New and Noteworthy

What is new and noteworthy in this book consists of these five elements: 1) the presence of gay and lesbian couples in Luke 17:34-35, 2) the postulated early career trajectory of Yoḥanan b. Zakkai in upper Galilee, 3) the key role of Philip the Tetrarch in resisting R. Yoḥanan's boundary-testing, 4) the formation of the *Same-Sex Pericope* (Luke 17:28-29 and 34-35) and 5) the independent Jewish and Christian "cover ups" of the Galilee Episode. The Luke 17:34-35 passage exists only because of the judicial confrontation between Philip the Tetrarch and Rabbi Yoḥanan b. Zakkai.

Many people concerned with religion and sexuality believe that Jesus never mentioned homosexuality, and technically speaking he didn't. But no one in the first century discussed *homosexuality* as such, anywhere, because the word didn't exist until the nineteenth century. Individuals in every generation have had to figure out where people *like that* fit in. Jesus' mention of homosexuals simply hasn't been on the radar. During the recent church debates over homosexuality, with Moses and Paul invoked regularly by gay-bashing fundamentalists, the best news in sight for Christian gays and lesbians seemed to be that Jesus wasn't chiming in. His seeming total silence on gays and lesbians was a blessing.

But then I looked more closely at those enigmatic "rapture" verses.

> I tell you, in that night,
> Two men will be in one bed,
> > one will be taken, and the other left.
> Two women will be grinding together,
> > one will be taken, and the other left.

> (Luke 17:34-35)

I heard that passage preached on plenty when I was young. But many years later an anonymous poster recommended looking up Luke 17:34 in the King James Bible. And—wow—I saw the verses in a whole new light. Maybe Jesus did mention homosexuality. That was 12 or 15 years ago.

Jesus did refer to gays and lesbians, their arrests, and their differing fates. With evidence from Josephus, the Talmud and the New Testament, I argue that Philip the Tetrarch resisted attempts by Rabbi Yoḥanan b. Zakkai to hold non-Jews accountable to Torah for homosexual behavior. Luke 17:34-35 are not prophetic or apocalyptic, but represent legal policy which honors the Roman practice of allowing subject tribes and peoples self-government. This Roman policy not only protects subject peoples from unnecessary imperial meddling, but also protects one people from another people's attempts to impose its laws on them.

Chapter by Chapter

Chapter one reviews Pharisaic political activity through Josephus and Talmud. Most Christians and Jews know about Pharisees through the lens of their religious tradition. This was my situation. In my imagination Pharisees had been a mixture of eighteenth-century East European rabbis with a little Joseph McCarthy sprinkled over John's gospel. Pharisees were not, as Josephus would have it, a mere philosophical school distinguished by Torah, resurrection, and table fellowship. From the narrative evidence in Josephus, the Pauline epistles and Acts, I argue that Pharisees were a diverse group of Jewish men using the primary means available for advancement in government and law enforcement. The means of advancement was the Law. Chapter one shows the variety of men called Pharisees, from the score-settling advisors of Queen Alexandra, to partners in messianic adventures such as Zadok the Pharisee, to instigators of suicidal spectacles such as Mattathias and Judas. None of them was afraid to get his hands dirty.

Chapter two focuses on Yoḥanan b. Zakkai as one of these typically political Pharisee and covers three major points. I have ignored the most purely legendary material, such as his encyclopedic breadth of knowledge, from flora and fauna to demonology and astrology. First, I highlight aspects of R. Yoḥanan that rabbinic Judaism found expedient to preserve. He believed that fear of God was superior to love of God as a motivation for obedience, focused on capital punishment, urged destroying everything connected with sexual transgression, and defended the practice of cross-species execution to a deliberately misnamed magistrate. Second, you will see that the truncated account of his time in Galilee (*Mishnah Shabbat* 16:7) actually accomplishes three things: it eliminates the embarrassment of his Galilee record, contains a potential wealth of legal information and broaches a doctrine of Law Enforcement Culpability. Third, I explain his legal role in the Galilee Episode.

Chapter three, "Gays and Lesbians in Luke," demonstrates the presence of two gay and lesbian couples in Luke 17:34-35. I document the sexual idiom of a key element in each verse, the words *bed* and *grind*. I discuss Old Testament antecedents, contemporaneous usages in Latin and Greek, and uncounted subsequent usages across language groups and across time. This was necessary to refute suggestions that modern American slang meanings were being imposed on first-century *koine* Greek. In addition to verse 34's time of day reference, suggestive of sexual activity, I discuss the immediate context of the passage, verses 28 and 29, where Lot and Sodom are discussed in some detail. The same-sex theme is not only verbally present in verses 34 and 35, it is present contextually in the Sodom discussion, all carefully written without a hint of condemnation.

Chapter four moves to "The Galilee Episode" itself and to gospel persecution. I discuss Philip the Tetrarch, Rome's appointed ruler, his major formative experiences, his geopolitical situation and his governing priorities. I also discuss familiar gospel passages about persecution, with contemporary parallel phenomena including "catch and release" and binational same-sex couples.

Chapter five, "Making the Same-Sex Pericope," explains, step by step, how and why Luke 17:28-35 was composed. Starting with the oldest layer (the Q source) I explain why an anonymous scribe duplicated the Noah story point by point, which duplication has long puzzled scholars. The scribe edited a key word (a *field* became a *bed*), then added a three-word phrase ("*in that night*") in order to clarify the grounds for arrest. I argue that subsequent scribes, knowingly or unknowingly, muddied the clarity so painstakingly achieved.

Chapter six explores some reasons why we missed the gays and lesbians in Luke 17 for so long, including concerns about stoking antisemitism, the habit of harmonizing the gospels, and the demand for a univocal Bible.

In terms of this journey, I began my research where chapter 3 begins, with Luke 17:34, then verse 35, then the context of chapter 17. From there I looked at criticisms of King James renderings made by nineteenth century churchmen, then at the Q Source. About this time, I learned of Yoḥanan b. Zakkai, a Pharisee whose time in Galilee overlapped the years traditionally attributed to Jesus. Rabbi Yoḥanan is the legendary founder of rabbinic Judaism, a political and legal figure in Galilee, Jerusalem and Yavneh who escapes the notice of most Christians.

Where I came from, no one commonly discussed how, in the time portrayed in the gospels, Pharisees were primarily involved in politics and law enforcement, so I looked into Josephus to help set the stage. For the sake of clarity, I begin the book close to where I ended my research.

Jacob Neusner, now deceased, was a rigorous contemporary scholar who stripped away as much legend from the Yoḥanan b. Zakkai material as possible. I base my understanding only on material vetted by this meticulous rabbi. His detractors criticize him for his prodigious publication record (over 900 books written and edited), but his early work, these analyses of Yoḥanan b. Zakkai and the Pharisees, have not been widely assailed with controversy. (The strongest anti-Neusner objections seem to be raised against his translation of the Talmud, which among other offenses apparently contains profanity such as the "F" word.)

An Uncontroversial Thesis

The basic thesis argued in this book is in some ways quite unremarkable. Prior to Rome's destruction of Jerusalem, Jewish leaders sought to strengthen their hold on Palestine through more vigorous law enforcement, especially laws against sexual transgression. These attempts were notably resisted when Jewish leaders attempted to enforce Torah prohibitions on gentiles, and a Rome-approved official forbade what he considered an illegitimate expansion of jurisdiction. This is the core of the present thesis and, were it not for the evidentiary sources and the original "cover-up," there is almost nothing objectionable in it.

There have been three important pieces missing from the story: 1) the motive for the persecution recorded in the synoptic gospels, 2) the identity of the chief persecutor, and 3) the story itself. There isn't one. To my knowledge, there is no discernible historical narrative of the events I postulate. But despite the absence of a *narrative*, clues to the events survived in three unsurprising places: the New Testament, the Talmud and Josephus. The role of the Pharisees as law enforcement is preserved in all three sources, their role in executions—all three sources. The undeniable presence of R. Yoḥanan b. Zakkai is preserved in the Talmud in two ways, first in the positive form of his personal character and legal interests, and in the mixed form of his Galilean service record, which is remarkably sanitized yet remarkably informative. In the New Testament evidence of Pharisees as law enforcement is found in the synoptic gospels and in the career of the rabbi Saul of Tarsus.

Pre-Crucifixion persecution is evident in the gospels, but its motivation has always been a bit murky, considering the thoroughgoing Jewishness of the canonical Jesus, and how long it took for Jews and Christians to come to a parting of the ways. That mystery dissipates, however, after examining Luke 17. The gay and lesbian presence becomes clear you see the relationship between 1) the Lot account of disaster in Luke 17:28-29, 2) the same-sex couples and their separation in Luke 17:34-35, and 3) the two uncritical occurrences of Sodom in Luke17:29 and 10:12. All testify to the significance of gays and lesbians in the persecution referred to in the synoptic gospels. Gay and lesbian couples were targeted in the Torah-based Clean-Up-the-Galilee Campaign of

Yoḥanan b. Zakkai, the most important Pharisee in first-century Galilee.

The Great Separation of Luke 17:34-35, a puzzle for Bible readers for twenty centuries, slowly becomes intelligible.

> I tell you, in that night,
> Two men will be in one bed,
>> one will be taken, the other left.
> Two women will be grinding together,
>> one will be taken, the other left.

The arrests took place in Bethsaida and Chorazin. These cities were in Galilee, but on the extreme western edge of Philip the Tetrarch's territory. Philip's brothers, Herod Antipas and Herod Agrippa, ruled the other two regions, which were mainly Jewish. Philip's territory, however, was overwhelmingly Arab, and self-governing Arab tribes were not subject to Torah. Philip overruled one aspect of the Pharisaic campaign and required R. Yoḥanan to release the non-Jewish sexual transgressors. Otherwise he followed the Roman policy of respecting local laws and traditions, including how local population groups policed themselves.

Unfortunately, no narrative of these events survives. Writing an account of how Philip the Tetrarch rescued gay and lesbian gentiles from a Torah-based anti-vice campaign was not on anyone's agenda, not Josephus', not the Talmudic authorship's nor the gospel writers'. Most members of the gospel writing "teams" would have found the Jesus' interest in gays and lesbians awkward and embarrassing. The jurisdictional conflict between R. Yoḥanan and Philip was peripheral to the story of the Christ. In terms of Josephus' goals, documenting certain law enforcement techniques of Jewish leaders who survived the Temple's destruction was a tricky matter. The Talmudic authorship glossed over Jewish legal subjection to Rome as much as possible.

The motivations of the Talmudic authorship was complex. The picture of Yoḥanan b. Zakkai's career, its action, pragmatism and decisive compromises is ancient, heavily edited and muddled. On the one hand, after 70 CE his decision-making style during his transitional leadership at Yavneh was unilateral, ad hoc, and situational. It was opposite the eventual rabbinic emphasis on Torah-based rulings. Talmudic rabbis resorted to posthumously assigning R. Yoḥanan the title "Rabban," which title gave blanket justification to arbitrary decision-making under emergency conditions. On the other hand, at key junctures he yielded to Rome's hegemony. Escaping Jerusalem during the Roman siege is seen by some as the act of a coward. Being against war *during* a war is never easy. His acceptance of Roman hegemony was an embarrassment, a poor example, controversial and quite unpopular.

For those of you who may not know, Yoḥanan b. Zakkai is credited with saving Judaism after the destruction of the Temple State, that is, the destruction of Jerusalem and the Temple in 70 CE. Yavneh was a coastal city in the south, a refuge for Jews loyal to Rome during the First Jewish-Roman War. It was here, among priests, Herodians and the other Jewish aristocrats that Yoḥanan b. Zakkai laid the groundwork for the complex transition from a Temple-centered *state* to a Torah-centered *religion*. He had a hateful task, damned if he did and damned if he didn't.

Rabbinic Judaism and Christianity were born in the same time of upheaval. In both groups, the earliest leaders and decision-makers were subsequently granted special titles which justified to posterity their founding actions: *Rabban* and *Apostle*. The earliest conflicts in both groups were papered over: the leadership transition in Yavneh and the leadership conflicts in the early church (Gal. 2:11-21; I Cor. 1:12; 3:4). Rabbinic Judaism and Christendom also tried to downplay and ignore problematical details, and engaged in what today would be called damage control, image management, or cover up. Discernible evidence of

Jewish and Christian damage control concerning the same episode is visible regarding something which occurred in Galilee, specifically in the area surrounding Bethsaida. The Talmudic authorship virtually ignored the embarrassing policy defeat of R. Yoḥanan, and the gospel writers effaced the sexual identity of gays and lesbians whose presence is preserved in Christianity's founding documents.

Pharisees in Josephus and the Talmud

In Jewish history, the Pharisees were important actors in the centuries before and after Jesus. The picture historians have of the Pharisees comes from three sources: the Christian gospels, the Jewish Talmud, and the historian Josephus.

The four canonical gospels evolved in a period of 100 to 200 years, a time of struggle and uncertainty which ultimately resulted in the victory of Christendom and the survival of Judaism. In the New Testament the Pharisees are portrayed as key players in politics and law enforcement. The gospel authorship wrote with pastoral, apologetic and expansionist goals.

The Talmud was written and edited over a period of about 500 years. During this time of turmoil and redefinition, the Talmudic authorship coped with the collapse of the Temple state and labored to channel Jewish energies away from the volatile nationalism that had precipitated temporal disaster and instead toward the Torah discussion and observance which was the avenue of national expression left to them.

Josephus is for us the most accessible historian for this place and period. His best-known works are *The Jewish War* (c. 75) and *Antiquities of the Jews* (c. 94). As a Jewish general he prepared for the Roman invasion of Galilee, designing defensive fortifications for those Galilean cities which resisted Rome. Josephus surrendering to Vespasian in Jotapata (Galilee) in 67. After serving as a Jewish general he was defeated and served the Romans as an interpreter. Reviled as a traitor by surviving Jews, he denounced Jewish independence advocates (whom he labeled Zealots), and many of his accounts are unique. Neusner explains the reliability of Josephus thusly,

> While we have to attempt to uncover the development of rabbinic stories, we may take for granted that the account of Josephus underwent no similar extensive revision and reworking by later historians. Admittedly, there were some interpolations, but in the main we have what Josephus actually wrote. We know who he was, we are able to locate his particular biases, and his writings do not involve a century of revision by other hands.[4]

When I began my investigation of the historical Pharisees for this project, my understanding was limited to the New Testament. My takeaway as a pastor-wannabe was profoundly cautionary: there but for the grace of God go I. Pharisees were a warning against hypocrisy, professionalism and self-seeking, against petty arguments over words. In the last decade or so my understanding has deepened through my study of the Pharisees, the Galilee and Yoḥanan ben Zakkai. Guides such as Elias Bickerman and especially Jacob Neusner made my trek into Talmud territory less intimidating.

Elias Bickerman (1897-1981) was professor of classics at Columbia University and researcher at Jewish Theological Seminary. As a careful scholar with a high reputation Bickerman wrote,

> The Pharisees of the period of 100 B.C.E. must not be imagined according to the pattern of the peace-loving teachers of Jabneh who were preaching harmony two centuries later. Early Pharisaism was a belligerent movement that knew how to hate.[5]

Jacob Neusner was an author, translator, professor and ordained Conservative rabbi[6]. He asked,

> Why did the politics of the day lead to bloodshed? What made the Pharisees—supposedly a "school"—murder their opponents, just as some of them had earlier been murdered? Clearly,

Josephus's story of what the Pharisees did exhibits a disparity from his account of what they believed. Belief in life after death ought not to have produced civil war.[7]

The statements of these scholars are consistent with the picture of the Pharisees left us by Josephus.

Four Episodes of Pharisee Political Activity

Four episodes illustrate the violence of politics and governance in first-century Palestine, with exclusive focus on the Pharisees. The four episodes, occurring in a space of a little under 200 years, are 1) the reign of Queen Alexandra (76 BCE-67 BCE), 2) the Eagle Incident (4 BCE), the Quirinian Census Revolt (6/7 CE), and 4) the obscure 9th of Adar Episode (c 66 CE).

The first three episodes are the most familiar, taken from the works of Josephus. Because of their familiarity and accessibility, I will cover them less thoroughly than the 9th of Adar. This fourth episode was memorialized in an unobserved fast and is not mentioned by Josephus with that label. In rabbinic writings, the event seems to travel incognito as 9Adar.

Reign of Queen Alexandra (76 BCE – 67 BCE)

Salome Alexandra was the wife of Alexander Jannaeus, a king of the Hasmonean dynasty whose reign was notorious for violent conflict. Alexander resisted the influence of the Pharisees. During his reign a civil war lasted six years and cost more than 50,000 lives. In a major incident in the Temple precincts, more than 6,000 Jews were slain by Alexander's troops. According to Josephus, in one particularly gruesome event 800 rebels were crucified at one time, and their wives and families were killed before their eyes as they hung on their crosses.

When Alexander died, his wife ruled alone as queen. According to Josephus, Queen Alexandra had a reputation for piety and wisdom, and took the Pharisees as advisors. In addition to increasing her army and arranging for more mercenary troops, she executed many of the advisors who had counseled her deceased husband to kill Pharisees. She reportedly gave the score-settling group a free hand in dispatching their opponents.[8] Josephus is a key source for the events of Alexandra's eleven-year reign. Neusner writes, "Under Alexandra Salome, the Pharisees killed anyone they wanted, and eminent citizens took refuge with Aristobulus, the heir apparent."[9]

Of these episodes, Alexandra's reign was the most congenial for Pharisees. They were her official advisors. They were violent, but their level of political violence was acceptable for the age and had precedent in Torah. The Pharisees were invited into government by the queen and achieved what seems to have been their ideal political arrangement: advisors to power, but not controlling the levers directly.

Judas and Matthias: The Eagle Incident (4 BCE)

The independent Hasmonean dynasty was followed by the compromised Herodian dynasty. The Herodians were overt puppet rulers directly appointed by the Emperor of Rome. Herod the Great was king in Judea from 37 to 4 BCE. In his waning days, his opponents took advantage of his sickly condition. While not labeled by Josephus, he described specific agitators as having "a reputation as profound experts in the law of their country." This is Josephus' standard description for Pharisees. A pair of militant Pharisees, Judas b. Sepphoraeus and Matthias b. Margalus, influenced many zealous young disciples. The Pharisees scorned the symbol of Roman domination hanging over the Temple's main gate. The golden eagle was a constant reminder of Jewish submission to Rome and had been placed in a very public place.

> This [eagle] it was which these doctors now exhorted their disciples to cut down, telling them that, even if the action proved hazardous, it was a noble deed to die for the law of one's country; for the souls of those who came to such an end attained immortality and an eternally abiding sense of felicity; it was only the ignoble, uninitiated in their philosophy, who clung in their ignorance to life and preferred death on a sick-bed to that of a hero.
>
> While they were discoursing in this strain, a rumor spread that the king was dying; the news caused the young men to throw themselves more boldly into the enterprise. At mid-day, accordingly, when numbers of people were perambulating the temple, they let themselves down from the roof by stout cords and began chopping off the golden eagle with hatchets.
>
> The king's captain, to whom the matter was immediately reported, hastened to the scene with a considerable force, arrested about forty of the young men and conducted them to the king. Herod first asked them whether they had dared to cut down the golden eagle; they admitted it.
>
> "Who ordered you to do so?" he continued.
>
> "The law of our fathers."
>
> "And why so exultant, when you will shortly be put to death?"
>
> "Because, after our death, we shall enjoy greater felicity." (Josephus, *Wars* 1.648–653)

"The young men and their teachers were burned alive." [10]

In Palestine, hostility to the appointees and taxes of the Romans continued, as did the agitation of the Shammaite[11] Pharisees to stoke resentment. Steve Mason wrote that the Eagle "incident indicates just how militant and non-pacifist individual Pharisees could be."[12]

Judas the Galilean & Zadok the Pharisee (6/7 CE)

We saw during the reign of Queen Alexandra the Pharisees in their preferred role, exercising power in an advisory capacity, as counselors to those in power. In the Eagle Incident we saw, as portrayed by Josephus, two Pharisees leading a group of disciples in a symbolic and suicidal attack on a Roman target. In this third incident, we have a Pharisaic priest mentioned as the second leader of a temporarily successful revolt. According to Josephus, in the tax revolt against the census of Quirinius (6/7 CE), Judas of Galilee was the main figure. The situation between Judas and Zadok the Pharisee is roughly comparable to a revolutionary movement with two wings: one military and one political. Zadok the Pharisee was the ideology guy, standing side-by-side with the messianic military figure Judas the Galilean. This was thirty years after Queen Alexandra took Pharisees into her government as advisors, a little over a decade after the Eagle Incident, and about sixty years before the Great Revolt against Rome that resulted in the destruction of Jerusalem and the temple. Zadok the Pharisee gave this messianic kingdom its Tanakh bona fides. This pair led their force of militants (zealots) and established a short-lived Jewish nation whose slogan was "God alone as king and ruler and His laws as supreme."

> In the year 6 or 7 C.E., when Quirinus came into Judea to take an account of the substance of the Jews, Judas, together with Zadok, a Pharisee, headed a large number of Zealots and offered strenuous resistance. Judas proclaimed the Jewish state as a republic recognizing God alone as king and ruler and His laws as supreme. The revolt continued to spread, and in some places serious conflicts ensued.[13]

This revolt was not known for being especially bloody, but some people have a way of not yielding power peaceably. The messianic kingdom of Judas and Zadok was put down by the Romans in short order.[14] These three examples illustrate the spectrum of Pharisaic political activity. It ranged from working within a Jewish dynasty, to asymmetric defiance and suicidal direct action, to a rebellion practical enough to proclaim a fleeting independent Jewish government.

Didactic summaries of the Pharisees are necessary, but they inevitably over-simplify. Despite Josephus' self-acknowledged biases, his picture of Pharisee leaders suggests a wide variety of personalities. Some Pharisees survived King Alexander Jannaeus, keeping a low profile, waiting for their opportunity, then worked as powerful advisors to Queen Alexandra. Other Pharisees, such as Judas and Matthias, died with their students in a blaze of defiant glory. One Pharisee, the Torah-observant priest named Zadok, co-lead a government overthrow to establish an independent Jewish government.

Pharisees were a broad segment of the population, mainly but not exclusively laypeople, who expressed their politics and governance using Torah. They were not a school or a sect as we use the words today. Pharisees were politically oriented men who were ambitious to see Jews alone rule Israel in accordance with "the Bible." Had they lived in second-Temple Palestine, Republican Jerry Falwell, Marxist Jose Miranda, and the Catholic Berrigan brothers would all have been Pharisees, not because they were religious hypocrites, but because they brought the Bible to bear on government. Christian leaders often leave uncorrected the notion that the Herodians (Mark 12:13; Mt 22:16) were concerned with political power but the Pharisees were only "religious." The difference? Pharisees legitimized their ambitions with Torah.

The 9ᵗʰ of Adar Episode (66 CE)

It seems that few gentiles have ever heard of the 9ᵗʰ of Adar, and for good reason. The 9ᵗʰ of Adar Episode comes to us with that label only through rabbinic sources related to an unobserved day of fasting. Religiously, the 9ᵗʰ of Adar is the opposite of Hanukah or Yom Kippur. The Talmud authorship was loath to provide much history as generally understood today. The "historical details" we have of 9 Adar, it seems, are disguised descriptions of the factional Jewish conflict during the siege of Jerusalem.

Early references to the 9ᵗʰ of Adar Episode are relatively general and do not provide realistic historical detail. These sources contain valuable information[15] regarding the magnitude of the conflict, and perfectly illustrate Talmudic obfuscation of historical events. One tells us, "These are the days that one fasts on from the Torah.... On the 9th of the month (Adar), they decreed a fast day because Beit Hillel and Beit Shammai had conflict with each other."[16] Another tells us, "On the fourth of Adar a dispute erupted between the students of Shammai and Hillel and many were killed."[17] Finally, we read in the Babylonian Talmud,

> They (Beit Shammai) thrust a sword into the study house and declared: "Whoever wants to enter may enter, but no one may leave!" And on that day Hillel sat in submission before Shammai, like one of the disciples, and it was as wretched for Israel as the day on which the [golden] calf was made.[18]

These three rabbinic sources differ in the level of detail the writers feel comfortable with. The first source is the most general, informing us that Hillelites and Shammaites had a conflict that was serious enough to merit a national day of fasting. The second tells us that the conflict resulted in fatalities. The third source elaborates the most, telling us that the 9ᵗʰ of Adar Episode approached a magnitude of violence ("thrust a sword") comparable to the bloodletting in the Golden Calf incident in the Torah (Ex 32-33).

Many rabbis were embarrassed to acknowledge that Jews would kill other Jews. Various strategies are used to mask the nature of the pre-revolt controversy over how to deal with the Roman occupation. First, the Romans are nowhere named in the texts; the occasion of the 18 Decrees is left unspecified. Second, instead of describing conflict of unknown duration resulting in thousands of fatalities, a fictitious event was created with details supplied by many sources. The Pharisee Josephus himself describes often violent political factions under the heading of "schools." Likewise, rabbinic sources talk about a sword in the "school house," about taking a "vote" and one group outnumbering another and about "enforcing" the 18 Decrees. Third, excuses are generated with the phrase "God forbid." There were later rabbis who were appalled at the internecine conflict. Unorthodox Jews such as the Karaites were more willing to air the dirty laundry of the ancients.

Self-censorship can be protection from enemies who would use history as a pretext for violence and persecution. This was a major impetus during subsequent centuries of Christian ascendency. Another impetus for self-censorship was to guarantee that future generations had fewer "bad examples" (whether Zealous or compromised) to follow.

The loss of national autonomy and a lengthy military occupation made it essential to suppress "bad examples." A basic feature of the post-70 rabbinic agenda was to make independent, confrontational action more difficult, more problematic. A key part of that agenda was to exalt desirable examples and precedents to prominence. When you want to teach your people to stop rebelling and insisting on national freedom, you don't exalt historical examples of people who rebelled against imperial power, refused to surrender, and acted unilaterally.

The 9th of Adar illustrates the passionate, violent mood in Judea and Galilee during the Great Revolt. It differs from the previous three cases we looked at in that the violence was not directed outward, at Rome or Rome's puppets, but inward, at other political factions. As repackaged by rabbinic sources, the 9th of Adar Episode was a domestic disturbance, an internal matter. The internecine struggle was not the sort of behavior the rabbis at yeshiva Yavneh could promote, but as guides for the Jews and their posterity, they could not ignore the roots of destructive internal conflict. So-called Shammaites were willing to kill other Jews over the issue of resistance, and so-called Hillelites were willing to die for the sake of their pragmatic survival strategy.

Later sources (several manuscripts of the *Megilat Ta'anit*) report that 3,000 Pharisees lost their lives, possibly relying on unwritten discussions or extrapolating from the book of Numbers. The declaration of a fast on the 9th of Adar indicates the gravity and magnitude of the episode. The 18 Decrees resulted from the episode, mandating an extreme separation of Jew and gentile.

A recent account of the sources for the 9th of Adar Episode was published by Rabbi Daniel Roth, American-born director of the Jerusalem-based 9Adar Project, in a resource titled "The Story of the 9th of Adar told through Disagreements."

Distant secondary discussions of the 9th of Adar Episode agree that the conflict occurred shortly before the Great Revolt. In 1871 Isaac Hirsch Weiss wrote that the incident had to have occurred after the death of Agrippa I (44 CE). Heinrich Graetz believed the incident occurred on the eve of the Great Revolt in 66 CE.

Roth's sources can be divided into three groups. First are the laconic references to this conflict between the houses of Shammai and Hillel. There is no death count, only vague references. Second come a modicum of detail, although the source or method to determine that detail is not apparent. Finally come lengthy, post-Enlightenment discussions.

The militant Beit[19] Shammai was dominant prior to 70 CE. Beit Shammai was consistently vilified in the Talmud, its values characterized as separatist, confrontational and militant. After the destruction of Jerusalem by Rome, and later when Jews forbidden to live there, Beit Shammai was blamed. Beit Hillel was ultimately ascendant after 70 CE, after it wrested control of Yavneh from Yoḥanan b. Zakkai.

The 9th of Adar Episode demonstrates the militancy of the Jewish players in the story. It makes sense that the "pro-war faction" would be the most militant, violent and dominant in this "discussion." Josephus describes the political factions as "schools and philosophies." This rhetorical move is common to both the Talmud and Josephus in their attempts to downplay Jewish agitation for self-rule. As rhetoric, it was intended to minimize the bare-knuckle factionalism that caused internecine conflict in Jerusalem.

The 9th of Adar: An Allegory

I believe the 9th of Adar story is an allegory of the factional conflict which occurred

> **Pharisee Political Behavior 76 BCE to 66 CE (90 Years)**
>
> - **Queen Alexandra** (76-67 BCE)
>   - ■ Uncompromising
>   - ■ Violent
>   - ■ Torah-Based
>   - ■ Practical Success
> - **Eagle Incident** (4 BCE)
>   - ■ Idealistic
>   - ■ Suicidal
>   - ■ Torah-Based
>   - ■ Practical Failure
> - **Judas the Galilean and Zadok the Pharisee** (6/7 CE)
>   - ■ Idealistic
>   - ■ Messianic
>   - ■ Torah-Based
>   - ■ Practical Failure
> - **9th of Adar Episode** (66-70 CE)
>   - ■ Fanatical
>   - ■ Fratricidal
>   - ■ Torah-Based
>   - ■ Practical Failure
>
> © 2018, Ronald Goetz

during the siege of Jerusalem. There is one obvious clue. In the school house version of the 9th of Adar, the Shammaites announce, "Whoever wants to enter may enter, but no one may leave!" This is virtually identical to the Zealot position during the Siege of Jerusalem, allowing Jews to enter the city, but not to flee. Couching bloody historical events in the language of the schoolhouse seems plausible. Real world politics is a schoolhouse for a nation. This violent struggle among the factions is satirized in Monty Python's 1979 film *Life of Brian*.

I believe the 9th of Adar is an allegory of the internecine conflict during the Siege of Jerusalem, picturing Beit Shammai placing a sword in the schoolhouse. This describes how the militant faction of John of Gischala employed coercion during the siege to prevent Jews from fleeing the city. If this hypothesis is correct, this is testimony to the political essence of Pharisees prior to CE 70, and consistent with the oft-observed anti-historical tenor of the Talmud. This interpretation of the 9th of Adar this way is not essential to understand the picture of Pharisee politics, but is indicative of the Talmudic avoidance of more straightforward history.

The 9th of Adar Episode is eloquent testimony to the political character of people called Pharisees prior to the destruction of Jerusalem. The Jews there varied from moderate to radical. Jerusalem was a real-world school house, and the earnest factions were labeled Hillelites and Shammaites.

From the cursory review of Josephus' Pharisee episodes, we see that the Pharisees were political and their political action was widely varied. The Torah is a big, flexible book. The strategies and tactics of Pharisees ranged from persecuted critics during the reign of King Alexander Jannaeus to trusted advisors under his wife Queen Alexandra. Pharisees subsequently had their unexceptional revenge on political enemies. Two Pharisees, Judas and Matthias, inspired the suicidal and symbolic Eagle Incident. The Pharisaic

Priest Zadok partnered with Judas the Galilean and established a short-lived messianic government.

If the 9 Adar episode allegorizes the deadly factional conflict during the Jerusalem siege, then rabbinic sources labeled moderate elements *Beit Hillel* and radical factions *Beit Shammai*, and Jerusalem is Israel's real-world schoolhouse. If the 9 Adar episode represents the civil war for control of Jerusalem, then rabbinic sources implicitly labeled *all* the factions in Jerusalem *Pharisees*. On the other hand, if the episode does not allegorize factional conflict during the Jerusalem siege, then it represents an otherwise unattested violent internal Pharisaic dispute focused on the radical separation of Jews and non-Jews.

Next, we will look at a pivotal figure, the founder of Rabbinic Judaism. While specifics of this Pharisee's early career were thoroughly suppressed, the surviving outline of his governing principles and key issues give us insight into what characterized his early career.

Takeaways: Pharisees

1. Josephus is the historical source for Pharisees with the most interest in "actual" history and acknowledges his biases.

2. Josephus is the source for Pharisees with the least religious bias.

3. While Josephus rhetorically describes the Pharisees as a "school" of Judaism, the Pharisees in his narratives are uniformly political and vary considerably from one another.

4. Under Queen Alexandra Pharisees controlled the levers of power and had revenge on mortal enemies.

5. The Eagle Incident exemplifies how Pharisees could advocate symbolic and suicidal action of their followers.

6. Judas the Galilean and Zadok the Pharisee exemplify a short-lived independent Jewish state under Pharisee leadership.

7. The 9th of Adar Episode is an allegorical account of internecine conflict during the Siege of Jerusalem.

8. The 9th of Adar Episode demonstrates the political spectrum of Pharisees subsequently labeled Hillelites and Shammaites.

9. The 9th of Adar Episode uses the "schoolhouse" metaphor, which it shares with Josephus' "school".

Yoḥanan ben Zakkai

Y oḥanan b. Zakkai was one of the most influential Pharisees of the period, credited with the survival of Judaism. The Talmud suggests that the first decades of his career were discouraging and unfruitful. Concerning these years poignant legends developed concerning his wife, his son, and his exorcist-disciple Hanina b. Dosa. Also, there are multiple versions of his escape from Jerusalem shortly before the city was destroyed by Vespasian's army. This legendary material is covered with judicious impatience by Rabbi Jacob Neusner in several volumes on R. Yoḥanan, one of which is titled, *Development of a Legend: Studies on the Traditions Concerning Yoḥanan ben Zakkai.*[20]

There is one report about Pharisee Yoḥanan b. Zakkai which riveted my attention to him the moment I stumbled upon it. The first assignment of his career, which assignment lasted some eighteen years, was in the Upper Galilee between 20 and 40 CE. Overlapping the traditional years of Jesus activity in Galilee, Yoḥanan b. Zakkai was there. The Talmud is silent on why he was in the Galilee, but no matter his official capacity, he was almost certainly a Pharisaic representative of the Temple state. As we saw in Josephus, the consistent Pharisaic agenda was to increase influence on government officials. The New Testament tells us the Pharisees were involved in law enforcement and tax collection. The specific city mentioned as his place of residence is 'Arav, located some twenty to thirty miles from Bethsaida and Chorazin.

While the Talmud is silent on the circumstances of his presence, I refer to his judicial work with words such as posted and stationed.

Given the centrality of Galilee in the Jesus narratives, I was surprised that I had never heard of Yoḥanan b. Zakkai, a Pharisee of inarguable stature, who had lived two- or four-days walking distance from the Sea of Galilee. During all the stories set in Galilee, R. Yoḥanan would have been nearby. He could have been present for Jesus' healings and exorcisms, the accusations regarding his authority over demons, the sermons on the mount and on the plain, and the telling of parables described in the canonical gospels. R. Yoḥanan was not present for the Calling of the Twelve Apostles, but he could easily have incited the public scolding of the Pharisees.[21] This overlap of the traditional years of Jesus' ministry, the experience of Jesus' earliest audience and the presence in Galilee of Yoḥanan b. Zakkai, was the key discovery that compelled me to explore the official record of the reputed founder of Rabbinic Judaism.

I reiterate my debt to Rabbi Jacob Neusner, my guide to R. Yoḥanan b. Zakkai. In the early 1970s he published *First-Century Judaism in Crisis*.[22] I will introduce many of his conclusions regarding the character and teachings of Yoḥanan b. Zakkai. Neusner was convinced that much evidence regarding R. Yoḥanan was suppressed, and all of it carefully filtered. While I prefer to possess evidence to support an argument, sometimes I am forced to accept the testimony of authorities. When it comes to Talmud, I rely heavily on Rabbi Neusner.

The Pharisees at Yavneh, a "remnant" of the first Jewish-Roman war, survived at the pleasure of Rome. When zealous Jews gathered from all over Israel for their last stand, the fight-to-the-last-man Zealots had done precisely that, and the most militant Galilean leaders had been decimated. The militants were for the moment defeated, and the militants were blamed by surviving Jews for Jerusalem's destruction. Josephus blamed Zealots for provoking the Roman invasion, and the rabbis of Yavneh scorned these same "Shammaites" for their stubborn defiance.

During the first Roman-Jewish War, the Romans sent cooperative collaborators and non-resisters to Yavneh: Herodians, Hellenistic Jewish aristocrats, priests of the annihilated Temple state and the laymen who were expert in the law and traditions of the nation. One thing on their minds was consigning blame, another was their personal role in the Jewish future. While this was a pivotal era of upheaval, the turmoil took many decades to subside. The Kitos disturbances among Diaspora Jews (CE 115-117) was followed by the Bar Kokhba rebellion (CE 132-136).

Two Jewish traditions guaranteed continuous turmoil and hope. The first tradition was the major theme of the book of Judges, which showed how God raised up leaders to battle gentile oppression when the cries of the oppressed reached heaven. The Judges tradition was a non-monarchical, non-elitist, fully vetted rhetorical resource for the Jews, an egalitarian example. In wisdom and faithfulness God could raise up any individual of any gender to deliver the Jews from oppression, no matter how incapable, unwilling, unlikely or ungodly the person.

A second self-renewing tradition was Passover, the annual celebration of God's deliverance of the Jews from foreign oppression. Passover was based squarely on home, family and God, a celebration independent of any temple, priesthood or government.

Yoḥanan b. Zakkai was the chief Pharisee at Yavneh for one or two decades. There was no peaceful succession in place, no orderly transfer of power. Jacob Neusner emphasizes that all we have of R. Yoḥanan's official record is what his hostile successors preserved.[23]

> That his teachings and acts at Yavneh were limited to the handful reported by rabbinic tradition is hardly reasonable. What

is preserved of the legal record is clearly what the members of the court of Gamaliel II saw fit to recall.... the literary sources reveal almost nothing of the opposition he must have met or of the viewpoints of groups that opposed him.

We have…almost no way of knowing what an editor thought of any great issue, whether legal, historical or theological, because, for the most part, we know very little about what he omitted, neglected, or suppressed.

There are huge gaps in the record of a character so historically pivotal. His time in Galilee has been summarized to an incredibly brief note. The decades between his tenure in Galilee and his legendary escape from Jerusalem is a memory hole. Neusner wrote that

Omissions are noteworthy, for it was largely by suppressing data that the rabbis expressed their opinion of their opponents. I think it very likely that numerous sayings of Yoḥanan were not merely lost or forgotten, but rather suppressed.[24]

Obviously, Neusner is not the only person aware that significant silences can exist in a text. Literary theorist Terry Eagleton wrote that "what seems absent, marginal, or ambivalent about [a text] may provide a central clue to its meanings."[25] Not everyone is attuned to such absences, marginalization and ambivalence, but some people are in agreement with the goal of such marginalizing suppression. Because of bias, it is important not to automatically accept an individual's characterization of a case being "an argument from silence." For example, if a paragraph on the Nixon presidency did not mention the Watergate break-in, that absence would merit question and comment.

After years of study, Neusner saw that the record of his subject, the life and teachings of R Yoḥanan, was riddled with omissions and distorted by suppression. Some motives for suppressing data about the founder of rabbinic Judaism are clearly justified. If you felt that Ribaz set the sort of example that brought the destruction of Jerusalem and the Temple state, then that example had to be suppressed, sanitized and re-worked. In that regard, the legends of R. Yoḥanan are similar to the legends of Hanukah.

("Ribaz" is an acronym for R. Yoḥanan b. Zakkai. Acronyms are used as compact references to many significant rabbis: Rambam is the acronym for R. Moses ben Maimon (Maimonides); Ramban for R. Moshi ben Nachman; Ribaz for R. Yoḥanan ben Zakkai. I use Ribaz, Rabbi Yoḥanan and Yoḥanan b. Zakkai throughout this book.)

Rabbi-Professor Neusner is carefully critical of his rabbinic sources. His concern is considerably less with pastoral edification and considerably more with academic rigor.

> The rabbinical legislators show no keen interest in narrative, biographical, or historical problems, but take as their task the promulgation of laws for the government and administration of the Jewish community.

Throughout my discussion of R. Yoḥanan I generally follow Neusner's lead.

> When we turn to the rabbinic tradition about the Pharisees, we shall look for the basic agenda, rather than for exact details, of Pharisaic law and theology. Considering the nature of the sources in our hands, we have no sound alternative.[26]

We look for "the basic agenda" as opposed to "exact details." Neusner is, nevertheless, a conscientious guide. He laid out a treasury of evidence, but often refrained from directly stating some conclusions. One thing that stands out to this reader is his habit of saying that a certain conclusion is untenable, lists unanswered questions, thereby leaving a trail of bread crumb clues, but apparently offers no explicit conclusion.[27] Neusner's mantra was a corrective to naïve, uncritical acceptance of each and every tradition. He ruthlessly cross-examined every tradition. He is known for his mantra, "What we cannot show, we cannot know."

Despite unreliable records, relevant evidence regarding the career of R. Yoḥanan was transmitted by his successors. Using Talmudic evidence vetted by Neusner,[28] we can approach a general picture of R. Yoḥanan b. Zakkai. We have a record of his judicial philosophy, and the reputation indicated by stories passed on, what was felt appropriate to attribute to him. Finally, we have a "bullet-point" summary of his Galilee record which is deceptively brief.

Fear vs Love as Foundational Motive

Fear vs love is one key to understanding Ribaz. In contemporary language, this is the difference between a society primarily depending on social welfare for order and one depending on law-enforcement and coercion—the carrot vs the stick. In a wealthy society, the love-welfare end of social control is an easier sell than the law-enforcement/stick approach. At the risk of being overly simplistic, religion can emphasize love as a motivation but governing requires fear.

This makes Ribaz more understandable, more comprehensible, though a reader may still dislike him. He's hard and uncompromising, interested in results, in survival, not in warm fuzzies and likeability. His apparent ruthlessness and focus are as much a cultural value as a personal or moral one. It is practical. He will resonate for people possessing power and authority.

Yoḥanan b. Zakkai believed that the bedrock motivation for obedience was fear. In one Talmudic discussion of love vs fear as the motive for obedience to God, R. Yoḥanan is invoked, signaling the magnitude of the difference.

> Rabbi Yehoshua exclaimed, "If only Rabbi Yochanan ben Zakkai were still alive! [29] He used to say that Job only served God out of fear as per Job 1:8, 'a pure and upright individual

who fears God and shuns evil.' Now your student's student, Yehoshua, has taught that he was motivated by love!" [30] (Mishna Sotah 5:5b)

Underscoring the significance of the motivating force of fear for R. Yohanan, the following story appears in the Babylonian Talmud, Berakoth 28b.

When Yochanan ben Zakkai was lying on his death bed, his students requested a blessing. He replied, "May your fear of God always be as great as your fear of flesh and blood." When they protested that their fear of God should be greater than that of mere mortals, their revered teacher responded: "Would that you feared God as much as human beings! When a person commits a sin, he is worried that someone may see him, but he is not afraid that God witnesses his transgression." [31]

It might seem too great a leap from the personal piety of Job to a question of national governing policy. What we see in this "famous last words" deathbed scene is the retooling of a dominant political philosophy to serve later pastoral ends. Such retooling was a central post-70 Pharisaic task, to engineer the transition of Judaism from a Temple state to a non-governmental religion.[32] Early in Yohanan b. Zakkai's career, however, Rome's destruction of the Temple state was in an unforeseeable future.

Connection with Capital Punishment

Yohanan ben Zakkai reportedly had a lifelong concern with capital crimes. Tellingly, this connection has been subject to condensation. In a passage often cited in brief surveys of Ribaz we read,

The more a judge tests the evidence, the more he is deserving of praise. Ben Zakkai once tested the evidence even to the inquiring about the stalks of figs.[33]

According to Neusner, the disrespectful label "Ben Zakkai" indicates the original citation was critical of the rabbi's scrupulosity, and this criticism was transformed by making judicial thoroughness praiseworthy. The negativity of the reference shows that he was controversial early on, and that his association with executions was part of that controversy. Whether or not scrupulosity caused the original conflict is not the issue. The focus on scrupulosity does two things. First, it acknowledges his interest in capital punishment, and it also deflects our attention away from his involvement in executions. He was a prosecuting judge, not a defense attorney. His goal was to apply Torah to every person in Galilee. After the collapse of the Temple state, a zealous advocate of capital punishment would be problematical.

The death penalty is a pragmatic and essential mechanism of Torah enforcement. The sterner the penalty, the more authority and fear adhere to the enforcer of the penalty. It is totally congruent with fear as a motivator to obedience to God.

Defeats Opponents with Deception

Two stories about Ribaz illustrate the priority of winning conflicts without concern for ethics or notions of so-called fair play. The takeaway from both is that recognized interpreters of Torah may forcibly bend adversaries to their will, in one case by trickery and in the other dishonesty (by reneging on an agreement). Both episodes portray R. Yoḥanan in conflict with priests, one seemingly before 70 CE and one after. The principle is independent of the Temple's existence.

We have the account of Ribaz Cutting the Priest's Ear. By this act Ribaz disqualified the priest from functioning or benefitting from his status according to Leviticus 21:18-24,[34] which prohibits the service of a Levite with any blemish. The action of Ribaz amounts, if you will, to a sentence without trial, a "summary judgment."[35]

> And the story is told that a certain Sadducee waited out his sunset and came to burn the [red] heifer. But Rabban Yoḥanan ben Zakkai learned of it. He came and placed his two hands on him and said to him, "My lord, high priest! How fitting are you to be high priest. Descend, immerse yourself at once."
>
> He descended and immersed himself and came up. After he came up, he [Yoḥanan] cut him on the ear.[36]

The following post-70 episode portrays Ribaz tricking a priest into yielding a Temple prerogative (blowing the Shofar) to the new center at Yavneh by establishing a precedent. To establish the precedent, Ribaz reneges on an agreement. The saying, "Just do it, we can discuss it later," is precedent-based, hierarchical and militaristic.[37]

> Once New Year fell on a Sabbath, and Rabban Yoḥanan ben Zakkai said to the Bne Bathyra,[38] "Let us sound [the shofar]."
>
> They said to him, "Let us debate."
>
> He said to them, "Let us sound [it], and afterward let us debate."
>
> After they sounded [the shofar], they said to him, "Now let us debate."
>
> He said to them, "the horn has already been heard in Yavneh, and one does not reply [in debate] after an actual deed [= precedent]."[39]

This preference for an "actual deed" (a precedent) over "debate" (discussion, consultation) is significant. Given the habit of rabbinic writers of reading their present circumstances and goals retroactively into history ("It has always been this way"), and the new and innovative centrality of the Law, one could assume that Ribaz never felt ethically "tied" to Torah. Had he been so tied, it might have been unnecessary to replace him at Yavneh, and perhaps his disciple Eleazar would not have been excommunicated for his stubborn adherence to a different set of traditional ways of doing things.[40] I believe one of the reasons Ribaz was so comfortable legislating from the bench at Yavneh, issuing decrees and deciding cases pragmatically rather than through reasoned Talmud exposition (related to *Hora'at Sha'ah*), is because he had been doing precisely that in Upper Galilee for decades.

Ribaz's opposition to war with Rome probably follows this same pragmatism vs principle difference. Jacob Neusner wrote several volumes on R. Yoḥanan and concluded that his opposition to the war with Rome "so permeates the traditions that it attains the status of an axiom."[41] Elsewhere, you will often find rhetorical descriptors such as *pacifist, peace party* or even *peacenik* connected with him. These labels may have described his first-century position on war with Rome but are highly misleading if we take them as a philosophical orientation toward foreign affairs and domestic governance. Following the examples of Tanakh (the Hebrew Bible), Pharisees had no qualms about taking human life, either in foreign policy or in ordering the inner life of the Jews (read: domestic policy). Pre-70 CE Pharisees were hardline law-and-order people. Pharisees who opposed war with Rome were against this particular war, an unwinnable, suicidal war. They were willing to serve as advisors to unrighteous rulers so long as domestic policy was in their hands. Neither Yoḥanan b. Zakkai nor Pharisees in general were against violence, coercion, taking human life or the use of force.

Talmudic Reasoning and Sexual Transgression

As important as each piece of the R. Yoḥanan picture is, there is one critical feature that is most pertinent to his law enforcement activity in Galilee. Following Neusner's lead, I will discuss three accounts, one anonymous and two of R. Yoḥanan.

Each of the three accounts addresses the destruction of something connected with a crime.[42] The first and third explain the requirement to destroy a living animal involved in a crime, and the second explains the requirement to destroy inanimate objects connected with a crime. The crimes in the second and third cases are specifically sex crimes. The Torah generally applies to the behavior of Jews, not to animals or stones. These legal discussions broaden penal destruction to include oxen, beasts, wood and stone. Neusner places these accounts on two contiguous pages in his 1962 book *A Life of Yoḥanan ben Zakkai*.[43]

The first account is disguised, and presents Yoḥanan b. Zakkai as explaining to "Antigonus the Hegemon" the rationale for sentencing an ox to death along with its owner. The second account is anonymous and deals with the destruction of all the objects connected to sexual worship on a high place. Neusner suggests that R. Yoḥanan may have been behind this second account. The third and final excerpt portrays R. Yoḥanan explaining the rationale for destroying a beast along with the Jewish woman who approached it for sex. It is important to note that the attribution of two or even all three of these explanations to R. Yoḥanan b. Zakkai is not critical to this argument. If he did not author these explications, then there was something in his reputation that made the attribution sensible, believable. But two of the three attributions are specific.

It is important to note that the words *lesbian* and *homosexual* do not appear in this chapter of Neusner's *Life*, nor in the entire book. This would not the first time Neusner used a rabbinic rhetorical strategy without announcing it. He nevertheless comments, "The antonymic relationship to the *midrash* on the stones of the altar is obvious."[44] This refusal to name the unnamable may or may not share the motivations of Christian churchmen and translators discussed in later chapters.

In discussions of homosexuality and Judaism, especially when zeroing in on lesbianism in the Talmud and not in Tanakh, commenters often observe that lesbian sexuality is not addressed specifically in Tanakh and not for one or two hundred years in Talmud. Saul the Pharisee refers negatively to sexuality between women and between men. Paul does not include women in the Romans 1 passage because of his Damascus Road experience, but because of the legal extrapolation common to Jewish law enforcement officials.

Ribaz Explains Double Execution to a Prince

The "Antigonus the Hegemon" case contains no specific sexual content but does have several interesting features. The story has at least four applications besides its use in capital cases.

> Antigonus the Prince asked Rabban[45] Yoḥanan ben Zakkai, *"The ox will be stoned and the master also die* (Ex. 21:29). Why?"
>
> He said to him, "The accomplice of a thief is like a thief."
>
> When he went out, the student asked, "Master, this one you pushed away with a reed, but to us, what will you reply?"
>
> He said to them, "It is written, The ox will be stoned and also its master will die—the death of the ox is to be like the death of the master, for the death of the one is juxtaposed to the death of the other; just as the master dies after a fair trial with careful examination of the witnesses and twenty-three judges, so the ox dies with careful examination of the witnesses and twenty-three judges." [46]

On the surface, the narrative seems anachronistic, reading back into history the face-saving, unwieldy Talmudic 23-judge quorum for capital cases. Second, it posits an ignorantly incomplete question from a ruler symbolically named Antigonus. If the two-line Torah couplet were quoted in its entirety, such a question would be completely unnecessary.[47] Third, the passage portrays Yohanan b. Zakkai as concerned with fair trials, careful examination of witnesses and due process,[48] as though he were an ACLU civil rights attorney. Finally, it signals friction between two legal systems, one subordinate and one dominant.

The name of the *hegemon* (meaning dominant one or *prince*) is fictionalized. In addition to generals and others, there are three rulers named Antigonus ("worthy of his father"), all of whom died before Yohanan b. Zakkai was born: Antigonus (382-301 BCE), Antigonus Gonatas II (319-239 BCE), and Antigonus Mattathias II (d. 37 BCE). R. Yohanan lived during the Herodian Dynasty. The intended audience may have had a sketchy grasp of history, but when it came to writing history, it was didactic utility that was paramount.

If the account represents an actual incident involving Ribaz, there are two possible candidates for the "dominant prince" in Galilee. One is Herod Antipas and the other is Philip the Tetrarch. Herod Antipas is better known to gospel readers, but Philip seems the likely candidate for one very good reason. Bethsaida was in his territory. In 30 CE he dedicated Bethsaida Julias, a fortified port which counterbalanced his brother's seaside city Tiberias.[49] This was Philip's building project, who ruled the Arab tribes directly east of the Sea of Galilee.[50] Philip the Tetrarch is probably the hegemon who required an explanation from Yohanan b. Zakkai about executing an "ox."

The episode involving "Antigonus the Hegemon" reflects the humiliating experience of a puppet state. It models saving face throughout. Rather than enshrine this humiliation in writing, a brief "exchange" between leaders is proffered, and the subordinate official is portrayed as an expert instructing his disciples. There is nothing geopolitically or religiously damning about communicating with a foreign ruler, no dangerous precedent, although the word *hegemon* carries with it the idea of dominance. As written, the hegemon is superficially deferential in asking R. Yoḥanan to explain a point of law. For all we know, they could have been chatting over coffee, not embroiled in a jurisdictional dispute.

The case under discussion seems rather minor, putting down a lethal animal. Under normal circumstances, a government could require a legal hearing, but many situations allow an authorized person to impound and destroy an animal administratively. In this case, an elaborate quorum of twenty-three judges is required to put an ox on trial. This scene of Ribaz answering to a government ruler, then outlining an elaborate capital trial to his pupils, is significant. First, it communicates the reality of a subordinate relationship with an absolute minimum of precedent-setting. No submission to a hierarchically superior figure is acknowledged. But secondly, using the necessary legal technique of lesser to greater reasoning, it is likely that the defendant in the off-stage trial is not an ox at all, but a person who, in the eyes of someone's law, is quite unlike the "owner" of the "ox."

Explaining a human execution is not the only point of this Talmudic discussion. This case has been efficiently composed for judicial multitasking. First, it is a precedent for communicating with gentile officials, but does not record a precedent of *accountability* to gentile officials. Second, the bulk of the passage illustrates a teacher explaining the law to his disciples, fulfilling a didactic purpose. Third, the passage illustrates how multiple rhetorical explanations for an event can be offered to various audiences.

Finally, the story of Ribaz and the Hegemon relates to capital punishment. It contains an example of antonymic minor-to-major reasoning. Such reasoning is key to the legal interpretation of seemingly insignificant laws and rulings. It allows for analogical comparison statements: "If God decreed death for that, then how much more certainly for this!" The story of Yoḥanan b. Zakkai explaining a point of law to a ruling prince applies to the execution of gentile sexual offenders.

Destroy Every Thing and Every Person

The second excerpt from Neusner justifies the Torah command to destroy everything connected with sexual worship at the high places. The main justification for destroying the sexual paraphernalia of the high places is *confusion*. To tolerate their continued existence will "confuse" people. The legal significance of the passage, the overt, didactic application of minor to major reasoning, is illustrated at the end. The destruction of the inanimate objects of high places is the minor case; executing human beings and the temptation they present (*confusion*) is the major.

> The *dorshe hamurot* [51] used to say, *You shall surely destroy all the places where the nations whom thou shall dispossess served their gods, upon the high mountains and upon the hills, and under every green tree; you shall tear down their altars, and dash to pieces their pillars* (Deut. 12:2-3). How did the wood and stones sin? But on account of them there came upon man confusion, and therefore Scripture said, You shall destroy their altars. And behold it is a deduction: If in the case of stone and wood, which have neither merit nor demerit, neither good nor evil, because on their account confusion comes upon man, Scripture said to destroy their altars, a man who causes others to sin, and turns them from the way of life to the way of death, how much more so will he suffer.

As previously noted, Neusner hardly comments on these passages. He may have thought their significance to his audience was self-explanatory. The preceding section explicitly equates the destruction of inanimate high place reminders of sexual idolatry with the destruction of human reminders of sexual transgression.

Execute the Woman and the Cow

Neusner's third excerpt is similar to the first two. The first excerpt deals with the destruction of an ox, the second with the destruction of inanimate objects connected with a high place. Finally, the third excerpt concerns the destruction of a beast-cow approached for sex by a woman.

> *And so too, if a woman approaches any beast and lies with it, you shall kill the woman and the beast, they shall be put to death, their blood is upon them* (Lev. 20:16). If the woman sinned, what sin did the beast commit? But because there came upon man confusion on its account, Scripture said to kill the beast, that the cow should not go into the market place and people say, "See, there is the cow on whose account so-and-so was put to death."

Yoḥanan b. Zakkai's commentary follow here.

> And behold, it is a matter of deduction: If in the case of the beast, who has neither merit nor demerit, because on its account man was brought into confusion, Scripture said to stone it, a man who causes his fellow to sin, and leads him from the way of life to the way of sin, how much the more (will he suffer).[52]

This episode is significant for several reasons. It illustrates the active interest of Ribaz himself in capital cases involving sexual transgression, and that he sought to destroy everything connected with such transgression. It is also related to the principle of minor to major reasoning. Here, by analogy, the beast represents a gentile sexual partner, who, though technically not subject to Torah, is subject to destruction by virtue of the confusion their continued existence would cause. Equating women with animals was not exceptional: Jesus called the Canaanite woman a *dog*, and Amos called certain noble women *cows* of Bashan. Approaching a beast for sex is identical with approaching any gentile, a male beast or a female cow, for sex.

Taken together, the thread of R. Yoḥanan's argument is as follows. Just as the brute unreasoning ox must die because of its involvement in a goring death, so also the phallic pillars and altar beds of the high places must be destroyed because of their association with the sexual rituals. To tolerate the existence of the ox or the altars and the pillars will allow and encourage further violations of the law. Following this same legal reasoning, the Torah demands the execution of any gentile, male or female, in a sexual relationship with a Jew.

These three sections demonstrate R. Yoḥanan's relationship to the analogical prosecution of sexual transgressors. The requirement for multiple witnesses is in Deuteronomy 19:15: "One witness shall not rise against a man concerning any iniquity or sin that he commits; by the mouth of two or three witnesses the matter shall be established."

Authority to Abrogate Torah

R. Yoḥanan's name is attached to something rather extraordinary: the abrogation of two provisions of Torah. The first cancellation is of Deuteronomy 21:1-7, pertaining to an unsolved murder in open country, and the second is Numbers 5:11-31, administering poisonous or bitter water to a wife suspected of adultery. The disuse of these Laws reportedly occurred when unsolved murders and suspicions of adultery became common.

> When murderers became numerous, the rite of breaking the heifer's neck ceased. When Eleazar b. Dinai came (and he was also called Tehinah b. Parishah) they changed his name to Son of the Murderer. (b) When adulterers became numerous, [the rite of] the bitter water ceased; and R. Yoḥanan b. Zakkai brought it to an end,

for it is written, *I will not permit our daughters when they commit whoredom nor your daughters-in-law when they commit adultery, for they themselves [go apart with whores . . .]* [53] (Hos. 4:14).

The mention of the Zealot Eleazar b. Dinai and the Hosea quote only seem like *non sequiturs* and are undoubtedly puzzles to be unraveled. But this contemplation of connections might not be necessary were the issue not Torah abrogation. Disregard of Torah cannot be tolerated merely because too many people ignore a law. The abrogation of Torah requires a suitable imprimatur, and Yoḥanan b. Zakkai had apparently become the go-to authorizer when decisions with neither precedent nor judicial reasoning required some sort of justification. Some form of authorization was required, no matter how insufficient or absent the reasoning. Mere tolerance or indulgence of transgression was unacceptable. At the risk of oversimplification, if your position required situational decision-making, citing Ribaz was always a good option. The title *Rabban* seems be a kind of retroactive authorization.

The Talmud credits Ribaz with officially abrogating the Rite of the Red Heifer and the Rite of Bitter Waters. He may have done this. If he did not, something about his reputation, personality or record allowed the Talmud authorship to drape him with the mantel of decision making not based on precedent or law. It was not an instance of *auctoritatem ex nihilo*. Any individual held responsible for the cancellation of even one jot or tittle of Torah would have demonstrated a similar audacity earlier in their career. Rather than enshrine a Galilean record of disregard of Torah, this capacity of Ribaz was used to justify post-destruction decisions. Today this species of decision-making is formally discussed under the heading of *Hora'at Sha'ah*, the Emergency Principle.

These two Torah abrogations are even more important for another reason. The Red Heifer and Bitter Waters rites were both Torah provisions that softened the law. From one perspective, these two examples of Torah leniency needed cancelling. In the hands of a good defense attorney they could provide the legal precedent for defending against virtually any law. Cancelling these two rites was potentially akin to a U.S. court overturning the Fruit of the Poisonous Tree doctrine or the Miranda decision.

We have evidence of R. Yoḥanan's deception to eliminate obstacles. Because his record was subjected to extreme suppression, we may wonder whether his actual deceptions were too problematical to record as precedents. Less difficult manipulations, such as forcing the priest to descend into the water, would suffice. Whether these were actual historical episodes or were artful creations is not the issue here. What is important is that in the centuries when the Talmud was written, their intended audience found the anecdotes believable.

Yoḥanan b. Zakkai's Official Record from Galilee

Sanitizing R. Yoḥanan's eighteen-year Galilean service record must, in part, be interpreted in terms of desirable judicial precedent. His role in the founding of Yavneh could not be ignored, but the Talmud authorship apparently felt that preserving his Galilean record was inexpedient.[54] So, his activities in Galilee, his 18 years of effective judicial, political and law enforcement work were summarized, and his culpability was disguised in the timid opinion attributed to him. The passage mentions his commentary on three minor decisions involving protective Sabbath regulation: covering an open flame in one's home, covering excrement with a dish and covering a lethal scorpion which was possibly in one's home.

> One may [on the Sabbath] cover a lamp with a dish so that it
> shall not scorch a rafter, and [cover] animal droppings to protect
> a child, or a scorpion so that it shall not bite. R. Judah said,
> "Such a case once came before R. Yoḥanan b. Zakkai in 'Arav,

and he said, 'I doubt whether one [who does so] is not liable to a Sin-offering.'"[55]

The following analysis may help us understand what the Talmudic authorship actually accomplished in their abbreviation of Ribaz's Galilean career. The passage in English translation does *not* say that R. Yoḥanan rendered the three Sabbath covering decisions. It says that "such a case once came before" him in 'Arav. Thus, he was involved in a case that in some way touched on the legal principles embedded in the three-case summary. As we shall soon see, the summary includes a minimum of ten distinct concepts, such as Sabbath, damage prevention, structure, dependency, etc., each of which undoubtedly merits lengthy treatment. Second, this Talmud portion contains a curious double-negative, "I doubt whether one is not liable." This double-negative is likely one of the keys to the passage.

The exegetical key to what many seem to regard as minor legal material is in the primer[56] for Talmudic legal interpretation and is called lesser-to-greater reasoning. Every individual word is important when interpreted as law and can be collated with any law or scripture passage in which that word or a related legal principle appears. We must remember that Torah is not primarily devotional or historical, but legal.

An Eighteen-Year Record, Condensed

Yoḥanan b. Zakkai's Galilean legal legacy was reduced to three kinds of threats one can *cover*: a lamp, animal droppings and a scorpion, and one's legal accountability in the act of enforcement. The distillation seems tailor-made as an exercise in Talmudic reasoning. The word *lamp* could refer to any sort of light, in this case, a false light or false teaching. In conjunction with the verse, "Thy word is a lamp unto my feet, a light unto my path," any belief, sentiment, teaching, or philosophy could conceivably be a false light, a deceitful lamp, which should be covered. Likewise, using Talmudic reasoning, *animal droppings* could be construed to include any residue, contaminant or uncleanness remaining from a person; it is a lasting influence even after an animal is gone and can cause unpredictable damage; a memory can create confusion, which can be damning. The summary has great utility by means of analogy. The idea that the painful sting of a *scorpion* is deadly when it penetrates the victim can be applied, again, to any belief, sentiment, teaching, philosophy, practice or failure to practice.

A *cover* can refer by analogy to anything that prevents further contact and influence; a *cover* extinguishes or kills a flame; it binds a perpetrator with an effective restraint, such as a rope. The energy expended varies in proportion to the size and nature of the thing "covered." As we extrapolate using minor to major reasoning, the *dish* could be anything appropriate to the thing *covered*: from a literal dish to manacles to an individual item in a pile of "dishes" used by the community to stone an offender to death. Using Talmudic reasoning, applied judicially with ingenuity, the *dish* could include any instrument necessary to effectively limit contact with, bind, or neutralize a threat.

The word *scorch* is by analogy equivalent to any action which burns, damages or influences for the worse. A *rafter* is part of a structure, it is protection, part of the man-made environment. Accordingly, any element of a protective structure, organization or system could be equivalent to a *rafter*. The word *protect* means to prevent further harm, future harm or potential harm. A *child* is one for whom a parent or guardian is responsible, someone who is dependent, helpless, vulnerable, needy or subordinate. A scorpion *bite*, in addition to hurting, damaging, infecting, breaking the skin and causing pain to a living being, also kills. The phrase *such a case* refers to any event that could be construed as similar or congruent using such comparisons.

While the Clean-Up-the-Galilee campaign could invoke such legal reasoning, the identical reasoning could also be used against the perpetrator of such judicial violence. The idea that during his tenure in Galilee a sage of R. Yoḥanan's eventual stature would be consulted only two or three times is patently absurd. The principal of multiple explanations illustrated by the story of Antigonus the Hegemon is informative here. While basic Talmudic legal reasoning was not given official expression until much later, we can see the utility and the justice of the Talmudic summary of R. Yoḥanan's Galilean legacy.

The idea of lesser-to-greater reasoning was foundational to Talmud application. An example of such reasoning would run something similar to this: "If God declared worthy of death a man gathering firewood on the Sabbath, how much more deserving of death is he who harvests his crops on the Sabbath." The actor, the action and the direct object may differ, but the penalty remain the same. According to many teachers, Ribaz rendered three decisions in Galilee: on the Sabbath one may use a dish to cover a lamp, animal droppings or a scorpion. The open flame threatens an environment or community (a house). The animal droppings threaten someone whose safety and well-being depend on you. The scorpion threatens any individual in the vicinity. Therefore, on the Sabbath, you may cover, bind, detain or extinguish anything, animate or inanimate, that threatens the structures of the community, the individuals under your care or protection, or anyone else. This statement is often cited to demonstrate his strictness. You may incur the penalty of a sin offering, but such is the cost of doing business. You do anything necessary to protect the individuals and community in your care.

While the focus of the passage seems to be the three kinds of threats, the three rulings or principles are not attributed to Yoḥanan b. Zakkai, but only associated with him. From what I can see, only the double-negative about needing to make a sin offering is attributed to him. In this passage, the only idea attributed to Yoḥanan b. Zakkai is that of *culpability* incurred in the performance of one's duties. Ribaz is only connected to responsibility and blame.

The "case" in which Yoḥanan b. Zakkai was involved could even have been his *own* case, involving an accusation or rumor of wrongdoing stemming from his decades in the Galilee. His defense seems to have been that he was protecting Israel, and he may have incurred blood guilt[57] as he *covered* a threat. Such culpability was unavoidable. His message to the Galilean leaders and council members whose verdict he needed was, "Bind and eliminate the dangerous transgressors in your homes and towns. They are a threat to your families and to all Israel." He mounted his culpability defense to the Hillelites who threatened to unseat him in post-70 Yavneh. "I had to bind them, even if I sinned. Woe to you if you bind them on the Sabbath, woe to you if you do not." Using the principle of "lesser to greater," or *kal v'chomer*, this is the background of the story of "The Scorpion under the Dish."

The three principles represented by the lamp, the excrement and the scorpion may represent the defenses Ribaz offered, not during a criminal trial, but in the struggle for control of Yavneh around 90 CE. This is not part of my argument, however. I am not a Talmudist. I do not attribute the following reasoning to a Talmudist. I offer the following material as a feasible application of

Talmud Portrait of Yoḥanan b. Zakkai

- Fear vs. Love as Basic Motivator
- Use of Capital Punishment
- Talmudic Reasoning and Sexual Transgression
- Secular Overlord Inquiry re: Ox/Owner Execution
- Destroy Everything Connected with Sexual Immorality
- Defeats Enemies with Deception
- Authority to Disregard Torah

© 2018, Ronald Goetz

the Talmudic summary of Yoḥanan b. Zakkai's tenure in the Galilee.

Three Cases of Covering with a Dish

We need to look at the three cases of covering with a dish and explain their possible application. In the lamp example, any false teaching falls under the rubric of "a fire that poses a threat" to Israel, and methods to effectively eliminate the threat are authorized. In the excrement example, any forbidden book or scroll falls under the heading of things which pose a danger to the people who depend on us. Finally, *covering* nonobservant nonconformists with a pile of stones will combat the false praxis. While the Talmud forbids executions on the Sabbath, Talmud formulas were not published until long after R. Yoḥanan was dead.

The dish seems to have been the symbol of enforcement. It symbolizes the least effort possible to eliminate a threat, to both Torah observance and the Temple state. An example of such an application, using the least effort possible to destroy an excremental forbidden book. Stoning with stones an apprehended male or female couple engaged in sex would require the least expenditure of energy on the judge's part. But work is work, and Torah enforcement is work, even on the Sabbath. As a necessary evil, enforcement of the law inevitably involves violating some social norm. Agents of the law inevitably violate standards of behavior that ordinary people are not authorized to violate. Agents of the law (Torah) must live with the results of their actions. In some contexts, this is called the cost of doing business, in others it is called an occupational hazard. A sin offering seems to be a slap on the wrist.

It seems likely that the actions of Yoḥanan b. Zakkai were so vigorous and lethal that he transgressed the Torah, possibly to the point of incurring blood guilt. I suspect much of the Tanaaitic[58] authorship of the Talmud saw itself as engaged in damage control when dealing with Ribaz. Tanaaim rabbis had a problem on their hands. R. Yoḥanan was undeniably heroic, and undeniably flawed. In emerging Judaism, few of R. Yoḥanan's Galilean actions were safe for emulation, they were unsuitable precedents. So, the rabbis crafted and edited that record to make it useful for a Judaism without land, temple or sovereignty.

The fire-excrement-scorpion summary of R. Yoḥanan's Galilean legacy outlined three areas of legal applicability: social structures, vulnerable dependents, and individuals. It is a "big picture" summary having less utility for individual cases than for broad legal doctrine. From my perspective as a generalist, the passage's legal contribution seems to regard the inevitability of transgression during the legitimate enforcement of Torah, and the responsibility of the enforcer to meet subsequent legal demands, specifically, sin offerings.

Galilean Record Processed and Expunged

We have a picture of a man whose temperament and reputation made it believable that he could officially abrogate two provisions of the Bible (Torah), a man who understood fear as a more effective motivator than love, who had a life-long connection to capital punishment, who explained to gentile magistrates the legal demand to destroy anything and anyone connected with sexual transgression. He was a pivotal figure in Jewish history, who took charge at Yavneh until he was ejected, who witnessed the collapse of the Temple state, who laid the foundation of Rabbinic Judaism. He was transformative, despite representing defeat, surrender and compromise. Ribaz was subservient to the Romans, yet abrogated Torah. Are we supposed to accept Ribaz's empty Galilean service folder? Is it believable that except for legends all we have are three decisions rendered in nearly twenty years of service as a young Pharisee? We will dissect that Galilean summary below.

R. Yoḥanan b. Zakkai is portrayed as a man with a mission, a sacred responsibility. It depended on where you stood relative to his duties whether he was a hero or a villain, a wild-West sheriff or a Judge Roy Bean. As a Pharisee, it was his responsibility to mount the postulated Galilean campaign, to eliminate Torah disobedience and gentile sin using all the means provided by law. In prosecutorial language, R. Yoḥanan had the means, motive, and opportunity to mount such a campaign. In the Talmud, Yoḥanan b. Zakkai is presented as a judicial hard-liner. Yet incredibly few of his judicial rulings are recorded. Thus, a Talmudic reputation exists, but few examples that reflect it, not the kind that satisfy the demands of today's historians. It is a classic case of telling but not showing. His strictness in Galilee is superficially restricted to Sabbath violation, supported by his comment on what some say were the only cases submitted to him during his tenure in 'Arav.

It may be that the picture of his melancholy failure in the Galilee[59] is a philosophical statement, an evaluation of his work in the light of Israel's eventual destruction. The case I lay out in these pages, if true, means that even in the Galilee R. Yoḥanan was a world-historical figure, but his brand of prosecutorial zeal is in view in Ecclesiastes 10:8. Recall some of Jacob Neusner's comments regarding R. Yoḥanan Talmud portrayal.

> Omissions are noteworthy, for it was largely by suppressing data that the rabbis expressed their opinion of their opponents. I think it very likely that numerous sayings of Yoḥanan were not merely lost or forgotten, but rather suppressed.

> That his teachings and acts at Yavneh were limited to the handful reported by rabbinic tradition is hardly reasonable. What is preserved of the legal record is clearly what the members of the court of Gamaliel II saw fit to recall.

We have, as I said, almost no way of knowing what an editor thought of any great issue, whether legal, historical or theological, because, for the most part, we know very little about what he omitted, neglected, or suppressed. [60]

While Neusner focuses on R. Yoḥanan's time at Yavneh, these comments are even more true of his career in ʿArav if the present thesis is correct. This presents us with some obvious questions. First, what kinds of data would merit suppression by Yavnean rabbis? Second, which of R. Yoḥanan's teachings and acts in Galilee would be unfit to recall according to the Yavnean rabbinic agenda? Third, what legal, historical, or theological issues regarding R. Yoḥanan would likely be omitted, neglected, or suppressed? And fourth, assuming we have evidence of a cover-up, who would benefit from such a cover-up?

Finally, I would underscore that it was the rabbis who embedded this legal summary in the context of ʿArav. I have not arbitrarily placed the comments of Ribaz on legal culpability in a Galilean setting.

The Galilee Episode

I have concluded that R. Yoḥanan b. Zakkai conducted a lengthy purification campaign during his eighteen years in the Galilee. We have seen evidence in Josephus of normal political activity on the part of the Pharisees, including lethal political retaliation, spanning the century prior to the period in question. Later we will see evidence of entrapment in both the Talmud and the gospels. There is evidence from the Torah enforcement perspective and some from the target community. In Luke there is evidence of nighttime raids, sudden and without warning. Evidence of pre-arrest coaching survives in that gospel as well. The gospels provide evidence of Pharisaic responsibility for the campaign, and for the use of deadly force.

While I don't believe R. Yoḥanan primarily targeted Jesus and the people he inspired, some phases of his purification campaign probably did. A Pharisaic campaign to bring law and order to the Galilee would not have had to target Jesus people, yet sweep up both leaders and fans. A small group with a distinctive ethos and charismatic leadership would have been an irresistible provocation for Yoḥanan b. Zakkai.

The Galilee region is relatively small, about 625 square miles, or 25 miles by 25 miles. A focused individual with a mission could make a major impact there in two decades. Some say that the single mention of Bethsaida and Chorazin in the Q Source is too slender to rely on as evidence to establish Galilee as the location of the composition of Q. Note that I am not here discussing the location of composition, but the location of certain historical events. Some say that gospel references to persecution and martyrdom are exaggerated, the whining of a few petulant counterculture types. The "vigorous debate" about whether Galilee was *either* a cosmopolitan mix of rural Jews and urban gentiles *or* a xenophobic Jewish ghetto is built on a false dichotomy.

Yoḥanan b. Zakkai:
Means, Motive, Opportunity

The means? One efficient way to convince a resistant population to conform to a shared ideology is to strictly enforce existing law, to "flex your muscle," to impose upon the population the discipline inherent in the accepted ideology. R. Yoḥanan was an expert in Torah with the prestige he shared with other Pharisees. He had experience in explaining Torah to gentile officials like Philip the Tetrarch. He used persuasion as an important method to enlist support for his campaign among local officials. Pharisees eschewed holding the reins of power personally and favored using civil authorities as instruments through whom to work. "Yoḥanan clearly considered himself the possessor of the legitimate internal autonomy available to Israel." [61]

His motive? To establish Torah in Galilee, a region sometimes called "Galilee of the Gentiles" (Isa. 9:1; Matt. 4:15). The Galilee was a region with its own, non-Judean religious identity from as far back as the days of Nehemiah and Ezra, a region about which R. Yohanan reportedly said, "Galilee, O Galilee, you hate Torah!" Galileans had little clout in the Temple state. In history, King Solomon apparently gave the gentile Hiram King of Tyre the territory of *twenty* Galilean cities as payment for temple building materials including cedar, juniper and gold (I Kings 9:11). After Solomon's death a civil war broke Israel into two separate kingdoms, and part of the Northern Kingdom was Galilee.

In the popular Christian mind, Galilee and Judea are merged together and treated as pretty much the same. This assumption is not just simplistic, it is incorrect. Galileans were never subject to Babylonian reeducation. Ezra, a Judean aristocrat, rudely rebuffed the Galilean offer to help rebuild the Jerusalem walls (Ezra 4:1-3). The Galilee area was annexed after military invasion by the Jewish Hasmonean king Aristobulus during his short reign (104-103 BCE). Annexation meant *forcible circumcision* for the males of Galilee. The name itself, "Galilee," did not honor one of the twelve tribes. The name is empty, meaning simply "region," akin to *zone* or *territory*. At times the Galilee was simply a zone where you could dump people you needed to relocate and reward them with land. I believe it was part of R. Yohanan b. Zakkai's task to continue Hasmonean forced annexation, bringing Galilee more firmly into the Jerusalem temple state tax base.

His opportunity? R. Yohanan lived in Galilee from about 20 to 40 CE. During this time, he saw the conditions that contributed to the era's numerous recruitment campaigns, including the campaigns of Judas of Galilee, Jesus of Nazareth and Josephus the general. He was posted to 'Arav, only a few days travel from

Bethsaida and Chorazin, the two towns where events occurred that brought Jesus' denunciation (Luke 10:13-15).

You will search in vain for a "story" recording Yoḥanan b. Zakkai's Galilee campaign. You won't find such a narrative in Josephus, the Talmud or the gospels. Telling the story of Yoḥanan b. Zakkai's domestic campaign to cleanse the Galilee of gentile pollution was not part of the agenda of any of these three sources. To tell this story would not have enhanced Josephus' goal of blaming Rome's Jewish problem on "the Zealots." The story would only distract from the life and work of Jesus the Christ. The embarrassing story would only acknowledge realities that had no utility for the rabbis. The fact that we have no narrative, however, does not mean that we have no *evidence*. We have evidence of a campaign in Galilee. Such historical evidence was neglected as such, and was repurposed, enhanced and expanded for rhetorical and literary reasons. Canonical John 21:25 acknowledges the incompleteness of the record.

The fact is that Galilee simply disappears from Bible history once Jesus leaves for Jerusalem. Outside the gospels, there is virtually no NT mention of the Galilee. Martin Hengel says that in terms of future church development, the importance of Galilee plummets to nothing. Paul and Luke agree that Galilee played no part in the further development of earliest Christianity. Paul mentions only Jerusalem and the communities in Judaea but does not mention Galilee at all; in Luke, Galilee appears only once and, on the periphery, in a redactional note (Acts 9:31). In other words, out-of-the-way, 'backwoods' Galilee quickly lost its significance for the further history of earliest Christianity and did not regain it even after the destruction of Jerusalem in 70 CE.[62] On the insignificance of Galilee, David C. Sim writes,

> [T]here is no external evidence at all for the existence of Galilean Christian communities. While Paul does refer to

believers in Jerusalem and Judea, he never mentions believers in Galilee. The sole reference in Acts to such Christians appears in 9:31 where Luke refers to the church throughout Judea, Galilee and Samaria enjoying a period of peace after persecution.... It is significant that, despite this reference to the church in Galilee, Luke says nothing about the origins or the later histories of these communities.... the fact that they left no impression on our sources means they were very few in number."[63]

Acts 9:31 begins, "So the church throughout all Judea and Galilee and Samaria enjoyed peace" (NASB). This section of Acts begins with Saul the Pharisee muttering threats, making arrests, and presiding over executions. His letters from Jerusalem authorized him to detain and deport followers of "the Way" in Damascus synagogues. Though Saul was obliged to obtain legal authorization to make these cross-border arrests of Jewish heretics, it seems certain that Pharisees residing in Galilee, such as Yoḥanan b. Zakkai, would not be required to obtain special authorization to enforce the law in their own territory. Performing law enforcement duties, Pharisees had a legitimate function, dealing with manpower and staffing issues, coordinating activities, and sometimes pressing jurisdictional disputes.

Both R. Saul and R. Yoḥanan dealt with problems of overlapping jurisdictions.[64] Saul had to obtain authorization to arrest Jews in Damascus, and Yoḥanan was required to justify to a gentile magistrate the application of Torah to a non-Jew. The two Pharisees differ in that there is no written account and no confession for Ribaz. On the other hand, for Saul the Pharisee we have both a narrative account and a written confession (Acts 8:1; 9:1; Gal 1:13).

As I have said, I am not a Talmudist, I do not attribute my conclusions to any Talmudist. Nevertheless, I agree with Jacob Neusner that the summary of Ribaz's tenure in Galilee is abbreviated. I have asked why. We use similar abbreviations today.

Depending on the context, the following list would raise few objections today: Miranda v Arizona, Brown v Topeka, Roe v Wade. I have interrogated the three-point summary and have noted what it specifically says in its mention of R. Yoḥanan and what it does not say. I assume that the gist of what I have written has been published some time, somewhere, in Hebrew.

The record of Ribaz was articulated by surviving leaders who themselves had driven the man from Yavneh. Legends appear where we would prefer more history. We do, however, know a few things. Yoḥanan b. Zakkai was present in Galilee at the same time as two others, Jesus of Palestine and Philip the Tetrarch. The Galilean work of Ribaz occurred before the Temple's destruction, while the Temple state was still relatively independent. I have so far described the politics of Ribaz in the light of the Pharisee narratives Josephus. A bullet-point outline of Ribaz's philosophy of pacification and law enforcement culpability survives. Despite Talmudic self-censorship we know of his interest in capital punishment, sexual transgression between Jews and gentiles, fear vs love, decisive action, trickery and deceit and the inevitable culpability of law enforcement and the judiciary.

In the first chapter we looked at examples of Pharisaic politics. We saw them when they were successful (as advisors to Queen Alexandra) and when they were visionary but practical failures (the Eagle Incident). We also got an idea of the Talmudic refusal to document what they considered bad precedents. This refusal was strategically effective but has not made the historian's task easy. In chapter two we looked at a Pharisee—Yoḥanan b. Zakkai—whose legendary story at the siege of Jerusalem is preserved in multiple versions, whose role in establishing Rabbinic Judaism at Yavneh is undisputed, but accurate details of which are apparently difficult to determine. His official record is consistent with a vigorous law and order approach to governance. Now we turn to the perspective of the targets of Pharisaic law enforcement. The absence of a narrative of R. Yoḥanan in Galilee does not prevent us from discerning the central features of his campaign. We will begin with the targets of Pharisee law enforcement, sexual transgressors.

Takeaways: Yoḥanan b. Zakkai

1. Yoḥanan b. Zakkai (aka Ribaz) is credited with helping Judaism transition from a Temple State to a religion.

2. Yoḥanan b. Zakkai's time in Galilee is almost totally eradicated.

3. We only possess information about Ribaz that his hostile replacements in Yavneh saw fit to preserve.

4. The only opinion attributed to Yoḥanan b. Zakkai from his Galilee tenure involves the culpability often incurred by those who obey (and enforce) Torah.

5. Ribaz believed that fear was superior to love as a motivation to obey Torah.

6. Ribaz showed a career-long interest in capital punishment.

7. Ribaz defeated opponents using deception.

8. Extending Torah application with lesser-to-greater analogy (*kal v'chomer*) was a major legal tool.

9. Ribaz justified to Antigonus the Hegemon the reason for executing an ox along with the woman who approached it for sex.

10. Using *kal v'chomer* the "ox" was probably a stand-in for any gentile approached for sex, including gentile lesbians.

11. Yoḥanan b. Zakkai brought charges of capital sexual transgression against two mixed-ethnicity same-sex couples, which required Philip the Tetrarch's ruling.

Gay & Lesbian Targets in Luke

> I tell you, in that night,
> there shall be two men in one bed;
>   the one shall be taken, and the other shall be left.
> Two women shall be grinding together;
>   the one shall be taken, and the other left.
> (Luke 17:34-35, KJV)

Many people concerned with religion and sexuality believe that Jesus never mentioned homosexuality, and technically speaking he didn't. But no one in the first century discussed *homosexuality* as such, since the word didn't exist until the nineteenth century. But same-sex attraction and activity did not suddenly spring into existence with Karoly Maria Benkert's coinage of a word. Discussing "homosexuality," Plato wrote that it is only

> regarded as shameful by barbarians and by those who live under despotic governments just as philosophy is regarded as shameful by them, because it is apparently not in the interest of such rulers to have great ideas engendered in their subjects, or powerful friendships or passionate love—all of which homosexuality is particularly apt to produce.

Plutarch wrote as well:

> The noble lover of beauty engages in love wherever he sees excellence and splendid natural endowment without regard for any difference in physiological detail.[65]

Unlike Plato and Plutarch, Jesus' mention of homosexuals simply hasn't been on the radar. During the recent church debate over homosexuality, with Moses and Paul regularly quoted by gay bashing fundamentalists, the best news in sight for gays and lesbians seemed to be the fact that at least Jesus wasn't chiming in. His apparently total silence on gays and lesbians was a blessing.

We have asked the question, *did* Jesus refer to same-sex couples in Luke 17. I believe verses 34 and 35 refer to a male couple and a female couple whose dwellings were raided during the night. One person from each pair was prosecuted and the other released. Luke 17 contains recognized symbols for same-sex activities for Jews and possibly for Romans. The Sodom story was a Jewish cultural marker by which Jewish readers knew that homosexuality was being discussed. Similarly, there was a Roman cultural symbol in the text, the lightning bolt and the eagles. In the past I understood these to symbolize Zeus and Ganymede. I now believe that they describe the involvement of a key regional ruler, Philip the Tetrarch, who continually traveled about his territory administering justice like an itinerent circuit judge.

First comes Luke 17:34-35. We need to look at the verses individually and in their immediate context. A few verses earlier, in Luke 17:28-29, Jesus is recorded as recounting the Lot and Sodom story, and that Genesis story contains the element of same-sex rape. Here in Luke we have two men in one bed, then two women grinding together, with no mention of rape. If either of these verses appeared in isolation, then it would be difficult to argue the presence of a sexual idiom. But with the iconic Hebrew story of same-sex activity immediately preceding, and the possible sexual content in the following verse, then sexual activity in verse 34 then becomes much more likely than mere sleeping or eating on a couch. This is far from eisegesis.

Rendering Verse 34

In Luke 17:34, there are two basic English renderings possible for ἔσονται δύο ἐπὶ κλίνης μιᾶς. Either "there will be two men in one bed," or "there will be two in one bed." If those few words were the only evidence for a same-sex theme in Luke 17:20-37 then this case would be quite weak. It could be a toss-up. But this is far from the only evidence.

Objections to the King James rendering of Luke's "two men in one bed" correctly include the fact that the word *men* is not present in the Greek text. There we find δύo (two), but none of the possible Greek words for men. All things being equal, in a contextual vacuum, the Greek word δύo could mean two men, a man and a woman, or two something-or-others. But the verse does not exist in a vacuum. It is preceded by the iconic Old Testament story of same-sex rape and is followed by another suggestive line of poetry. This is the very essence of context. Anyone who, in support of the *two will be in one bed* rendering, argues that the Greek word *man* does not appear in verse 34 should seriously consider the following exhortation. You must never again accuse someone else, "You're taking it out of context." In context we have the Sodom story, two men in one bed, and two women grinding together, at night.

Blame the Reader, Blame Society

Since 1611, countless ministers preaching on Luke 17:34 have had to disavow the sexual content of verse 34.

> "Just because two men are sleeping in the same bed doesn't mean something bad is going on. I used to sleep with my brothers when I was young, and we weren't gay. Also, it was common for travelers in ancient Israel, as well as for poor laborers, to share the same bed."

Why has a disavowal of the sexual content in Luke 17:34 been necessary in the tens of thousands of sermons on the rapture? Very simple. The details of the section include the destruction of Sodom: Lot, fire and sulfur, details the audience would connect with two men in one bed at night. What is not clear, perhaps until now, is the reason. Why mention Sodom, why mention two men in one bed, two women grinding—at night, if not to condemn them?

Exegesis: Antecedents

If you are familiar with evangelical Bible exegesis, then you know that one common practice for interpreting the Greek scriptures is to find antecedents in the Hebrew Bible. For example, if you wanted to explore the meaning of "Son of Man" in Matthew and Luke, you might begin with the 14 instances of "Son of Man" in Ezekiel and the one in Psalms.

There are antecedents for Luke 17:34, but I've only found two Old Testament references to two men laying together with unmistakable sexual content. The first assumes an implied male reader, of course.

> *Thou shalt not lie with a man, as with a woman:*
> *it is abomination.* (Lev. 18:22)

> *If a man lie with a man, as he lieth with a woman,*
> *both of them have committed an abomination:*

> *they shall surely be put to death;*
> *their blood shall be upon them.* (Lev. 20:13)

The Scripture says to let a matter be confirmed by two or three witnesses (Dt. 19:15; Matt. 18:16; II Cor 13:1). Leviticus 18 deals broadly with sexual purity, and Leviticus 20 with penalties for holiness code violations, which are often capital crimes. Both witnesses condemn same-sex male intercourse.

Before rushing to deny possible sexual content in Jesus' remarks, it seems more responsible to follow some of the normal procedures for doing exegesis. Proper exegesis begins with examining the passage's 1) context, 2) antecedents and 3) literary form. If such thoroughness is too demanding, then it might be best for some people to forgo future comment on Luke 17:34-35.

Exegesis: Context

Regarding the context of δύο, we've already noted the discussion of the destruction of Sodom. Now I don't believe the "sin" of Sodom was necessarily homosexuality. But there are many today who do. To this day the virtue of hospitality and generosity is greatly valued in the middle east, and lack of hospitality is grounds for personal and social rejection. Lack of hospitality can take many forms. In most places, raping tourists would be considered inhospitable. I think most of the Jewish believers among Luke's readers may have believed that as well.

Omniscience is unnecessary to know that when reminded of the Sodom story, the audience would have man-on-man sex in mind and might easily assume something sexual between the *two men in one bed*. First conclusion: the context of the masculine *duo* suggests sexual activity. We will now look at poetic parallelism.

Exegesis: Form

Although Hebrew poetry appears in many places in the Bible, five entire books in the Hebrew Bible are poetry. Job is one of them, the others are Psalms, Proverbs, Ecclesiastes, and Song of Solomon. The prophets are written in a mix of prose and poetry. In English, traditional poetry rhymes. In Hebrew poetry, instead of rhyming, there are parallel or complementary thoughts. The ideas can be roughly the same, they can show contrast, there are many varieties. Many Bible readers are used to taking each line or verse as a separate idea and neglect the meaning embedded in parallel thoughts. Hebrew Poetry as such was basically unrecognized until a full-length book treatment was published in Latin in 1753.[66] Examples:

> The words of a man's mouth are deep waters,
>   The fountain of wisdom is a bubbling brook.
>   (Prov. 18:4)

> In the place of judgment—wickedness was there,
>   in the place of justice—wickedness was there.
>   (Eccl. 3:16)

> Praise the LORD, all his heavenly hosts,
>   you his servants who do his will.
> Praise the LORD, all his works
>   everywhere in his dominion.
>   (Ps. 103:21-22)

Hebrew poetry is quite flexible. It is no wonder that about 75% of the Hebrew Bible is written as poetry. While there are no entire New Testament books written as poetry, there are several notable pieces of poetry in the Greek Scriptures.

In the poetry from Psalms above, note how lines 1 and 3 parallel one another, and how lines 2 and 4 are separately parallel. The Couples Couplet is poetry, and, after two introductory clauses, is structurally similar to the Psalm above.

> I tell you, in that night,
> Two men will be in one bed,
>   one will be taken, and the other left.
> Two women will be grinding together,
>   one will be taken, and the other left.

Understood as poetry, it is even more clear that two parallel lines describe sexual activity, and two lines describe disparate treatment.

Linguistic Exegesis:
The Beds of Luke and Leviticus

There is an interesting linguistic relationship between Luke's "two men in one bed" and the prohibition in Leviticus about a man laying "with a man as with a woman." The Hebrew idea of "lay with a man as with a woman" is not the literal language of the text. In the Hebrew, this idea is expressed with an idiomatic phrase. In Leviticus 18 and 20, what is translated as "as with a woman" is closer to "*beds of woman*" (אִשָּׁה מִשְׁכְּב). Recall that in Luke Jesus says, "In that night, two men will be in one bed." Within the prohibition against same-sex male intercourse in 18:22 and 20:13 is embedded the word *bed* (*miš·kə·ḇê*). This is one of the few verses where the Hebrew word *miš·kə·ḇê* is not rendered *bed*, *couch*, or *lay*.

אִשָּׁה מִשְׁכְּב

beds of   woman

The verbal connection of Leviticus 18:22 and 20:13 with Luke's "two men in one bed" is quite unmistakable. The word *bed* appears in all three places, in the two Levitical witnesses and in the Couples Material.[67] Looking for the word *bed* in an English translation of the Leviticus 18:22 and 20:13? Good luck.

I used to assume that the absence of *bed* in Leviticus 18:22 in the KJV was due to the translators' use of understandable idiomatic English. Now I seriously doubt that. The Hebrew word *miš·kə·ḇê* is rendered *bed* or *beds* nearly thirty times. Only here is it rendered by the words "as with." The verse in the KJV reads "Thou shalt not lie with mankind, *as with* womankind: it *is* abomination." Something akin to *beds-of woman* would appear in the nearly identical verses Leviticus 18:22 and 20:13. It is strange that the *miš·kə·ḇê* would disappear entirely from both verses, considering the unmistakable sexual associations of bed.

And if you're wondering whether the word *bed* had sexual connotations when the KJV was published in the seventeenth century, the answer is yes. The connotations were as common then as they are today. The King James Version was published in 1611. Shakespeare wrote his plays at this same moment in history. In the following examples, the Bard uses *bed* and *bedded* sexually.

- He "would thoroughly woo her, wed her, and bed her." (*Taming of the Shrew*, I, 1, 149, c. 1592)
- "I have wedded her, not bedded her; and sworn to make the 'not' eternal." (*All's Well that Ends Well*, III, ii, 20, c. 1602)
- "Let not the royal bed of Denmark be a couch for luxury and damned incest." (*Hamlet*, I, v, 82-83, c. 1599-1602)

The word *miš·kə·ḇê* is generally rendered *bed* or some related word. While the word *bed* had sexual connotations when the KJV was translated, it is entirely missing from the prohibitions against male intercourse. In Hebrew the word is *miš·kə·ḇê*, and in Greek it is *klinēs*.[68] It's odd how words, as if by magic, appear and disappear in the history of translation.

Is *Women Grinding* Modern Slang?

Verse 35 has the second specific mention of same-sex couples, *two women grinding together*. The NASB, known for its literal renderings, reads *two women grinding on the same place*. Just as the word men does not appear in verse 34, neither does the word *women* appear in this verse. We know, however, that it is *women* who are grinding because of grammar. The Greek word *grinding* (ἀλήθουσαι) is a feminine participle.

When I began this research, I knew I couldn't simply import modern English slang into a two-thousand-year-old text. Such anachronisms are totally unacceptable, as many people have pointed out. At the beginning of my research I looked for Old Testament antecedents for the word *grinding*.

It turns out that in the Hebrew Bible, *grind* is an idiom for sexual intercourse in at least three places: Job 31:10, Judges 16:21 and Lamentations 5:13. Job uses *grind* idiomatically for sexual intercourse when he defends himself against his pious accuser-friends.[69] In prison, Samson is put out to stud for the wives of his Philistine captors. And in Lamentations, the mourner describes the sexual degradation of women of all ages, children and young boys.

By the way, I was puzzled by which label was appropriate for the word *grind* for a long time. I used to say that *grind* was "used sexually." Specifically, I called it a *euphemism*. I called it a *metaphor*. That was not quite correct. *Grind* can be used be sexually, but as an *idiom*, an idiomatic word. It is not poetry, it is not slang. It is how language is used.

Job 31:9-10

The Book of Job is written as Hebrew poetry. Hebrew poetry does not rhyme, but its couplets are parallel expressions, and its lines often have equal numbers of Hebrew words.

> If mine heart have been deceived by a woman,
> or if I have laid wait at my neighbor's door;
> then let my wife grind unto another,
> and let others bow down upon her.
> (Job 31: 9-10, KJV)

The second line of verse 10, "let others bow down upon her" is an idiomatic expression for sex. For the first line, "let my wife grind unto another," some translations supply a word such as "grain," allegedly for "clarification." But many translations simply render it *grind*. This latter rendering, simple and unadorned *grind*, doesn't attempt to dictate to the reader the "real meaning" of the words of scripture by insinuating a single meaning from an ambiguous text.

Other translations have striven to communicate the *meaning* of the metaphor instead of rendering it literally. For example, the 1535 Coverdale Bible reads,

> O then let my wife be another man's harlot,
> and let others lye with her.

Coverdale trades literalness for clarity and impact. In typical poetic form, both lines refer to sex. In this instance the Coverdale Bible is more similar to the Living Bible than the NASB. The Talmud understood this instance of *grind* in the Book of Job as an idiom for sex.

The various renderings of Job 31:9-10 are but one example of the trade-offs Bible translators must make when translating, especially regarding sexual language. Contemporary translators must balance goals which include literalness, readability and doctrinal utility. On top of this, they face the church's culturally defined desire for decency and propriety in the sacred scriptures. The demand for decency and propriety can also be described as a commercial concern.

Samson in Judges 16:21

The second example of *grind* as a sexual idiom is in the story of Samson. Samson was a resourceful warrior and a notorious womanizer. After Delilah's betrayal and his resulting capture, Samson was enslaved by the Philistines. Near the end of his life, the Book of Judges reads, "the Philistines took him, and put out his eyes, and brought him down to Gaza, and bound him with fetters of brass; and he did grind in the prison house" (Judges 16:21, KJV). The Talmud understood *grind* sexually, here as well as in Job.

"And he ground in the prison-house" (Judges 16:21) R. Yochanan said, "Grinding always refers to [sexual] transgression, as it says, "Let my wife grind after another" (Job 31:10). This comes to teach us that every Philistine would bring his wife to [Samson] in the prison-house so that she might be impregnated by him [and bear a son of Samson's strength].[70]

Captured and blind, Samson was "put out to stud" for the wives of Philistine nobles who wanted offspring who would inherit Samson's legendary strength. Once more we see that *grind* with the meaning of sexual intercourse was neither lewd nor obscene, though it may not have been entirely polite. It was the ordinary way that ordinary human beings spoke. It was the language of the common (koine) people. Jesus' statement that "in that night…two women will be grinding together" is clearly an acceptable, thoroughly Biblical idiom.

Lamentations 5:13

A final Hebrew example of the *grind* idiom is in the Book of Lamentations. The book describes Israel's horrific experience during its conquest by Babylon. The book mentions mothers boiling and eating their own children during the siege (Lam. 4:10; 2:20). Lamentations 5 describes the brutality of Babylon's conquering soldiers.

> Our enemies rape the women in Jerusalem
> and the young girls in all the towns of Judah.
> Our princes are being hanged by their thumbs,
> and our elders are treated with contempt. (5:11-12, NLT)

The devastation is completed in verse 13:

> They took the young men to grind,
> and the children fell under the wood. (KJV)

Impressionable young men and children were sexually assaulted. There seems to be a common unwillingness on the part of Protestant translators to clearly render the obvious sexual violation here. Catholic translators of the Douay Rhiems version made the meaning a little clearer: "They abused the young men indecently: and the children fell under the wood." The phrase "Taking young men to grind" refers to the rape of the young male population, which was a humiliation often inflicted on defeated enemies and according to many, despite penile penetration, had nothing to do with sex.[71] Man-on-man rape, and wartime rape in general, are well-documented events in the history of military conquest, even though many readers and non-academics don't know about it.[72]

There is an important comparison between the Couples Material in Luke and Lamentations 5:13. In Luke, two sexually charged meanings are arguably subtle: *two men in one bed*, and *two women grinding together*. In Lamentations, the subtlety is in the phrases *to grind* and *under the wood*. According to some scholars the Biblical word *wood* is sometimes associated with the penis, as it is in English.

Some people consider the sexual content of Luke 17:35 an interesting idea but get stuck on the idea that we're importing twentieth-century American slang into a first-century Greek text, a different culture in a very different age. While an increasing number of people note the possible presence lesbians in Luke 17:35, it isn't enough to simply *say* that the "two women grinding together" are lesbians. Insofar as "proof" is possible, you need to *prove* it. People who take Bible interpretation seriously require evidence. I have demonstrated that the word *grind* was an acceptable idiom for sexual intercourse in the Old Testament in at least three places (Job 31:10, Judges 16:21, and Lamentations 5:13), which would be enough evidence for many reasonable people. But Old Testament usage is, by itself, insufficient. I knew early on that I needed to demonstrate that *grind* was used sexually in the time of Jesus.

A Sexual Idiom in the Time of Jesus and Luke

I could hear a potential objection ringing in my ears. "You have no evidence that *grind* was used sexually in the time of Christ." That would be a valid objection. Starting out, I didn't have any evidence of such use, and if there was no evidence, I would simply be making an interesting but unpersuasive assertion. I was trained as a scribe. I know how scribes think.

Was there evidence to support my hypothesis? In 2009 it really was *just* a hypothesis. At that point I was nowhere near convinced that verse 35's "two women grinding together" were lesbians. At that point I knew that they could simply be two women grinding grain in their mills by candlelight. (Oops. Sorry about the anachronism. That should be "lamplight.") But I found the evidence. I said to my wife repeatedly, "Diane, this is astonishing, am I just being too damned clever?" My friend Idan Enright later said, "There is an embarrassment of riches."

The *Grind* Idiom in Four Ancient Languages

Grind was an idiom for sexual activity in at least four ancient languages: 1) Hebrew, 2) Sumerian, 3) Latin, and 4) Greek. I've already discussed *grind* in Hebrew, so I'll move on to the remaining three.

Sumerian

The Sumerian Empire lasted approximately 1700 years, from 3500 BCE to 1763 BCE. In Sumerian, the word *mú* has at least four interrelated meanings. In linguistics, multiple meanings are discussed as semantic expansion or lexical change. These meanings illustrate how one meaning can morph into other meanings. *Mú*'s closely related meanings are 1) to mill or grind, 2) well-formed, beautiful, plump; 3) shout, scream, roar; and 4) woman, female.[73]

The linguistic relationships among these meanings of *mú* are relatively plain. Each of the meanings is related to women, their appearance and/or sexual activity. Linguists have demonstrated that words pertaining to the activities of women frequently become sexualized. Something almost identical to the linguistic expansion of the Sumerian *mú* occurred in the Greek *mello*. The Greek word *mello* meant "to have sexual intercourse." *Mello* originally meant "grind."

Latin

In Latin, the word "grind," and the related word "mill," are both sexual idioms. The Roman poet Horace (65 to 8 BCE) used "grind" in his endorsement of brothels. Writing in Latin just decades before the traditional birth of Jesus, Plutarch writes:

> Once, when a noble left a brothel, "Blessed be thou for thy virtue!" quoth the wisdom of Cato: "for when their veins are swelling with gross lust, young men should drop in there, rather than grind[74] some husband's private mill." [75]

Notice that Horace uses both *grind* and *mill* idiomatically. His use of the words together shows that even with the word *mill* the possibility remains of idiomatic sexual meanings in *grind*. Horace's usage is significant because it is a Latin idiomatic use of *grind* for sexual intercourse just a few decades before the birth of Jesus.

Greek

While the evidence from Hebrew and Latin is persuasive to me, there is an example in classical *Greek* where "grinding the mill" refers to sex. This example is more to the point since the New

Testament came to us in Greek, not Hebrew or Latin. This example from secular Greek is also significant because it was written at the same time Luke was probably finalized. This example demonstrates that the words *grind* and *mill* were sexual idioms, in Greek, in the time of Jesus and Luke.

Plutarch (ca CE 45 to 120) was born near the Greek city Delphi and was Luke's contemporary. One of Plutarch's essays, "The Banquet of Seven Wise Men," is a fictional conversation among some famous men who lived around 650 BCE. After a brief lull in the conversation, Thales of Miletus speaks:

> This remark arrested the attention of the whole company, and Thales said jestingly…. "when I was at Lesbos, I heard my landlady, as she was very busy at her handmill, singing as she used to go at her work:
>
> > Grind, mill, grind;
> > For even Pittacus[76] grinds,
> > King of great Mytilene…."
>
> > ἄλει μύλα ἄλει
> > και γαρ Πίττακος ἄλει
> > μεγάλας Μυτιλήνας βασιλευων

In rhythm with her grinding, the landlady sings a bawdy work song[77]: "Grind, mill, grind." This song is described as representing "the rich Lesbian folk song tradition." [78] Whether the song dates to 650 BCE is not the point. What matters is that Plutarch uses the word *grind*, as a sexual double entendre, in a lesbian setting, in the last quarter of the first century CE, overlapping the probable years of the completion of canonical Luke.

Plutarch's story confirms that *he* considered the work song to be a "lesbian joke," since he says that Thales of Miletus told the story set on the Isle of Lesbos "jestingly." The historicity of the story itself is not at issue here. Plutarch's story contains an example of *grind* used sexually in a lesbian context in Greek in the time of Luke and Jesus.

Grind in Plutarch and Luke

The fact that Plutarch places the line "grind, mill, grind" on the Isle of Lesbos, home of Sappho, is significant. In the linguistic evidence from Hebrew, Sumerian, and Latin, there has been no specifically lesbian reference. But the parallels between Plutarch and Luke are perfect. The fact that the parallel usage is historically documented moves the interpretation from the realm of speculation to the realm of verifiable plausibility.[79]

Plutarch wrote his collection *Moralia* between 75 and 100 CE. These years overlap the estimated years of the final composition of the gospel of Luke, which range from the early 60s to sometime in the second century. Plutarch's double entendre was amusing and required no explanation for Plutarch's literate, first-century Greek audience. The sexual usage of *grind* and *mill*, used together, was common in Greek society during Luke's final redaction, and was likely used a lot earlier. As to whether *grind* and *mill* were first-century sexual Greek idioms, whether the words were used separately or together, or whether these meanings were familiar to literate Greeks, there is no room for quibbling.

Grind is Not American Slang

The sexual use of *grind* is not a wispy example of ephemeral American slang. *Grind* has been used throughout history with a sexual application. Yes, there are examples of slang that become popular for a few decades or centuries then dwindle into disuse (e.g. gams, groovy[80]). But this is not the case with *grind*. The sexual use of *grind* is an *enduring* usage, and as we shall see seems to be linguistically, temporally and geographically universal.

World-Wide Use Historical and Modern

Grind is used for sex in many contemporary languages, several medieval and renaissance languages, and in four ancient languages as well. The contemporary sexual use of *grind* includes Japanese,[81] Swahili,[82] Chinese,[83] Hokkien,[84] Arabic,[85] and German.[86]

In her book, *Female Homosexuality in the Middle East*, Samar Habib, former professor at the University of Western Sydney, thoroughly documents the history of textual representation of lesbians in Arabic. The word *grind* in its various forms appears repeatedly throughout the book as the normal word for lesbian love making. After discussing briefly its use in Cantonese, she writes

> It is amazing that this word—grinding – whether in English, Arabic, or Cantonese, can provide a cross-cultural, cross-temporal, not to mention multilingual identification of female homosexual activity.[87]

Moving further back in time, *grind* is used sexually in medieval Arabic,[88] Tocharian B[89] and Chaucer[90] and in the Shakespearean[91] and Stuart eras.[92] Patricia Simons, professor of art history at the University of Michigan, discusses the sexual use of *grind* in Classical Latin, French, Renaissance Italian, and Shakespearean English:

> The pestle was penile in morphology but action is key to its sexual meaning; it not only entered the mortar in a steady rhythm but its function was to grind. The friction and exertion of grinding, especially of milling flour or grating cheese, was sexually charged and relates to the medical as well as practical understanding of coitus.... Coitus was likened to grinding corn or grain between millstones to produce the white substance of flour, familiar in such languages as classical Latin (*molo*), Renaissance Italian (*macinare*), French (*moudre*) and Shakespearean English.[93]

As you can see, linguists have traced the sexual use of *grind* throughout Asia, Africa, and Europe.

Grind and *mill* were common sexual idioms in English from the fourteenth through the seventeenth centuries as seen in Chaucer (1343-1400) in *The Canterbury Tales* (e.g., "The Reeve's Tale," "The Wife of Bath's Prologue") and Shakespeare (1564-1616) (e.g., *The History of Troilus and Cressida*, I.1). Gordon Williams documents over twenty instances of sexual *grinding* in as many different works from the 1500's through the 1700's, establishing that the sexual use of *grind* was common and widespread, and not the creation of two literary geniuses.

People have legitimate concerns about anachronisms, and the temptation to read contemporary Western meanings into ancient texts, including when it comes to slang. We are accustomed to hearing that slang is temporary, fleeting and ephemeral. We are rarely exposed, however, to enduring usages like *grinding* unless we're students of Chaucer's *Canterbury Tales*. When we realize that *grind* was idiomatic for sex in Middle English, as well as in contemporary German, Chinese, Swahili, and Japanese, we begin to realize that the sexual use of *grind* is not a transient phenomenon restricted to contemporary English.

There are at least three reasons for the universality of the *grind* idiom. The first two reasons are 1) possible linguistic influence and 2) the historical durability and utility of the idiom. The third is the fact that, in a sense, it simply isn't used as a metaphor. I can grind two rocks together, I can grind my teeth, I can grind my fist into my palm. Sexual grinding is simply one more literal application of the word. In many languages there are words rendered in English as either *grind* or *rub*. The sexual use of the word *grind* is not figurative or poetic but is quite literal. During love making, two bodies literally *grind* against one another.

In this discussion of *grind* in ancient languages, I am reminded of the canonical story of the crucifixion of Christ, and the sign reportedly nailed above his head.[94]

> And a superscription also was written over him in letters of Greek, and Latin, and Hebrew, "THIS IS THE KING OF THE JEWS." (Luke 23:38, KJV).

From canonical Luke to the Rosetta Stone to the SALT Treaty, communicating in multiple languages has never been unusual.

When you remember that there is earthy language throughout the Bible, in both testaments (see skubala in Phil. 3:8, and Ez. 23:14-21), we begin to understand that the church's demand for regal, solemn, respectable language is not a consistently Biblical demand. Standards of propriety, of acceptable language, are culturally conditioned. The expectations of church culture are not necessarily in sync with the scriptures. What sounds vulgar and earthy today was an acceptable Biblical idiom. And where the original was likely vulgar, even obscene (e.g. Ez. 23:20), then so much more reason for an English rendering that preserves the original impact. The church's consistent hesitance to interpret Luke 17:34-35 correctly is not surprising. Christian pastors are often not vocationally comfortable with Scriptural earthiness.

By way of example, the love poem Song of Songs, commonly attributed to Solomon, is well known for its sensuous descriptions of romantic love. First century Israel may not have had the clinical, scientific nomenclature for sexual matters we have today, but they did have acceptable ways to discuss these things among adults.

When I was finally convinced by Plutarch's usage that the grinding was sexual, I was disgusted. For days I felt personal revulsion. Jesus, using gutter language. (You have an idea of what a prig I could be.) But it wasn't gutter language. The Hebrew books of Job, Judges, Isaiah and Lamentations use grind with its normal range of denotations. Jesus used ordinary, acceptable language to refer to lesbian love-making.

Obviously, not every Biblical use of the word grind is sexual. But truncating the word's semantic range is not acceptable. In the cultures reflected in the Bible, grinding was an acceptable idiom for sexual intercourse, close to the word screwing, but probably edgier than today's idiomatic phrase making love.

Compulsive Harmonization

In the debate over the presence of gay and lesbian adults among Jesus' earliest followers, textual differences between Matthew and Luke come up. Some insist that Matthew 24 makes a stronger "agricultural" [95] connection with *grind* than Luke 17. Whereas Luke simply presents two women *grinding*, Matthew narrows the reader's focus to this: two women "grinding at the mill." The main issues we need to consider are 1) the presence and absence of the word μύλονι (*mill*), and 2) the broader issue of harmonization. Here are the two verses:

> There will be two women grinding at the same place; one will be taken and the other will be left. (Luke 17:35, NASB)

> Two women will be grinding at the mill; one will be taken and one will be left. (Matt. 24:41, NASB)

This difference reminds me of two verses in the Beatitudes of Matthew and Luke, involving gospel-supplemented words, where the added word has theological significance.

> Blessed are you who are poor, for yours is the kingdom of God. (Luke 6:20)

> Blessed are the poor in spirit, for theirs is the kingdom of heaven. (Matt. 5:12)

In both the beatitudes and the couples material, Matthew adds material. Translators believe that ancient scribes were more likely to *add* words than they were to delete. Deleting words more often creates ambiguity, while their considered addition narrows meaning toward a focus not present in the originating materials.

Experience taught me there's a difference between being "poor" and being "poor in spirit." If translators were to insert Matthew's phrase "in spirit" into the gospel of Luke, there would be a legitimate outcry. Adding "in spirit" to Luke 6:20 for purposes of alleged clarification would be a deliberate attempt to *gloss* over a difference in theological emphasis between the two gospels, and would obscure the concern for the economically disenfranchised (poor) of Luke.

Matthew domesticates the content in "two women grinding together" in much the same way he spun the "Blessed are the poor" material. He added "in spirit" in one passage and "mill" to the other. Matthew 5:3 and 24:41 display the same impulse to tame and domesticate. Such differences among the synoptic gospels allow scholars to explore the concerns that are unique to the various gospel writing teams. For example, such differences allow students of the Bible to determine that the gospel attributed to Mark was written for a more Roman audience, the one attributed to Matthew for a mainly Jewish audience, and the Lukan gospel for a more gentile audience.

Some people say that such differences

The Same-Sex Theme in Canonical Luke

- The Centurion's Servant (Lk 7:1-10)
- The Beelzeboul Accusation (Lk 11:14-15)
- The Lot & Sodom Material (Lk 10:12; 17:28-29)
- The Zeus & Ganymede Symbolism (Lk 17:24, 37)
- The Couples Material (Lk 17:34-35)

© 2018, Ronald Goetz

allow scholars to notice that Luke places a special emphasis on social outcasts like women, the poor, lepers, tax collectors, and Samaritans. My thesis that Luke's Small Apocalypse may contain the theme of Jesus' acceptance of non-celibate gays and lesbians is consistent with Luke's emphasis on marginalized groups.

There is a corollary to the idea that differences between the synoptic gospels allow us to see differences in emphasis. The deliberate habit of harmonizing synoptic gospel accounts *obscures* differences in emphasis. This is especially true for people who depend wholly on the Bible in translation.[96] *Muloni* is the Greek word for *mill*. *Muloni* is present in the Greek of Matthew 24, but it is *not* present in Luke 17. The absence of the word *mill* in Luke 17:35 is significant, as significant as the absence of *in spirit* is in Luke 6:20. Only people naïve to the discussion of gays and lesbians in the Christian gospels would characterize this tinkering as innocent or objective. There is a potential difference between women grinding grain in a mill, and two women grinding together in the same place. And while there is an area of overlap, there is a difference between theology and history.

The Same-Sex Elements are Deliberate

The same-sex theme of Luke 17:20-37 is made up of four elements. Any one or two of these elements alone would not be enough to establish a *theme* of same-sex relationships in the section. Taken together, however, they suggest two things: a same-sex theme *and* its deliberate creation. We see deliberation in the fact that three of the four elements are not in the Q source but were added to what became the gospel of Luke. The three elements are close enough to one another, that we may surmise they were added to Luke as a block. The Sodom material, the reference to *that night* and *two men in one bed* are in a cluster, and that cluster is unique to Luke.

One sign of the passage's careful construction is its parallelism. The story of Noah is common to both Matthew and Luke, but only Luke has the parallel Lot and Sodom cycle. The description of the *days of Lot* is structurally identical to the *days of Noah*, but there are two apparently insignificant differences. One difference is how those days are characterized. The details in the Noah account include how *they married wives, they were given in marriage*, but those details have been deleted in the Lot account, signaling awareness of altered social sexual arrangements. While the Sodom cycle has parallel construction with the Noah cycle, this difference is consistent with the proposed theme. In first-century Palestine, gays and lesbians didn't get married.

Let me state what the Lot story does *not* add to the passage. It does not add a theme of judgment—neither the word *judgment* nor God's necessary involvement is in the passage itself. It does not add the theme of the ordinariness of life before disaster occurs—that was present in the Noah cycle. It does not add the theme of actual disaster—that was also in the Noah cycle. It does not add the same-sex element to the passage—there are two same-gender couples present in the field and grinding together.

The Lot story may not add the same-sex theme to the passage, but it *does* add that element to the illustrating material from the Old Testament. The Sodom cycle brings to the passage precision and focus. Again, according to Ezekiel[97] the "sin of Sodom" was a self-centered neglect of justice, and the violation of the cultural demand for hospitality to strangers, which we don't take very seriously in the west. It is useless to deny the same-sex element (homosexual rape) which energizes the Genesis 19 drama, even though *theologically* it is subsidiary to the principle of hospitality. *Dramatically*, it is not.

Two elements of the gay theme (the Sodom cycle and the new location of the two men) were based on preexisting elements (one couple in the field and one grinding together). Of the preexisting elements, the Noah Cycle has no same-sex implications. The same-sex couples had no explicit sexual implications, although the unrecognized reason for their separation was probably clear to the earliest audience. Even together the Noah cycle and the women grinding were probably insufficient evidence to argue for a gay theme. In the transition from the earlier sources to canonical Luke, however, the number of same-sex elements in this small space leaps from two to six. We can reasonably conclude the Lukan same-sex theme was intentional.

Parallelism: One Taken, One Left

This final example is of parallel construction and nearly identical wording: *the one shall be taken, and the other left.* Depending on the interpreter, the Lukan Jesus might either 1) illustrate the Great Separation using two intimate same-sex couples, or 2) warn early followers of persecution by referring to the gay and lesbian couples targeted for nighttime raids. The separation occurs immediately before the climax of the passage. From a theological perspective, which is how the verses are traditionally approached, verses 34 and 35 contain a "moral of the story": lesbians and gays are not automatically condemned by God. When viewed traditionally, half the homosexuals are taken, and half of them are left. But this record was not originally theological and predictive. The material is historical and judicial.

We have identified the judicial and law enforcement agents involved (the Pharisees) and briefly surveyed some historical highlights. We have identified the agency head, discussed his later career, his areas of concern, and his philosophy of law enforcement. We have looked at some opaque defense evidence of alleged victims of oppression. But what exactly is supposed to have happened?

For me, it's taken a while to wrap my head around the political reality of Pharisees as opposed to the religious versions subsequently put forward by Jews and Christians. That difficulty is the result of the effective dual redefinition of Pharisees necessitated by the dissolution of the Temple state. It is easy to glide over the idea of making the transition from nation to religion, easy to feel dismissive of a religion's avoidance of historical facts. No one, however, has cornered the market on avoiding sticky details.

Takeaways: Luke's Small Apocalypse

1. In the Small Apocalypse of Luke 17 Jesus refers to gays and lesbians.

2. The suggestive word *bed* in verse 34 refers to the Levitical Holiness code prohibitions of male homosexual activity.

3. The sexual idiom *grind* of verse 35 is found several times in Biblical Hebrew as well as contemporaneous Latin and Greek texts.

4. The sexual activity in the passage take place *in that night*.

5. These sexual references in verses 34-35 are subsequent to the account of Lot and Sodom in verses 28-29.

6. Charges of sexual transgression were brought against two mixed-ethnicity same-sex couples by Yoḥanan b. Zakkai.

7. The Great Separation of verses 34-35 is based on a legal jurisdictional ruling by Philip the Tetrarch.

The Galilee Episode

When we acknowledge the possibility that the Luke 17:34-35 evidence may refer to gay and lesbian couples, various pieces of evidence become significant. The Talmudic evidence of the Pharisaic mandate to enforce prohibitions against same-sex practices became relevant. In Luke there are the two references to Sodom (10:12-13; 17:29), the Couples Material (17:34-35), and the Lot cycle (17:28-29). The fact that the same-sex couples in Luke were persecuted because they were homosexuals sheds light on many of the persecution elements in Luke's gospel. We understand more about division between family members (12:52-53), entrapment (Matt. 24:23; Luke 17:21) and raids ((Luke 17:34-35), trials before magistrates and citizen assemblies (Luke 12:13), prearrest coaching (Luke 12:1-3, 11-12), etc.

This convergence of synoptic gospel persecution texts involves many things. First, the sexual and ethnic nature of the crime (interethnic homosexual coupling). Second its geographic location (Bethsaida). Third, the legal jurisdiction (Philip the Tetrarch). Fourth, the fact of legal proceedings. And fifth, the differing dispositions of the defendants (*one seized* and *one left*). The responsibilities and goals of the prosecutor and the judge become relevant, and the sources of information retain their typical relevance (Talmud, Josephus, and the gospels).

Without Luke we would have no inkling that the arrests and trials even took place. We would have no understanding of the people arrested, why they were arrested, or the disposition of their cases. Without Josephus we would have less insight into the role and character of the Pharisees in general or Philip the Tetrarch in particular. Without the Talmud we would have considerably less insight into the depth and variety of Pharisaic law enforcement procedure. Neither would we have as much insight into their legal extrapolation of Torah in the area of sex crimes, the degree of their animus against same-sex practices, or the Pharisaic ideal of law enforcement discernible in the portrait of Yoḥanan b. Zakkai. Taken together, however, we have a reasonably complete picture. What follows is the essential Galilee Episode.

The Galilee Episode

Rabbi Yoḥanan b. Zakkai was located in 'Arav in Upper Galilee. His "jurisdiction" was over Galilean Jews, most of whom were under the civil jurisdiction of Rome-appointed Herod Antipas. There were some Jews in a small sliver of Philip the Tetrarch's jurisdiction in the towns of Bethsaida and Chorazin on the north shore of the Sea of Galilee. While comparatively little is known of Philip, he is mentioned in Luke 3:1. In the year 30 CE Philip's activities dramatically affected the politics in one of those cities. The political constitution of Bethsaida was changed, being elevated from ordinary town to imperial polis. With this change in legal status came a degree of uncertainty regarding the relative status of the city's inhabitants. In order to eliminate this uncertainty, and likely to establish a favorable precedent, R. Yoḥanan carried out raids and arrests of mixed-ethnicity same-sex couples in the cities of Bethsaida and Chorazin. This would have been consistent with Torah prohibitions against male homosexual practice, the legal extrapolation of this law to include female transgressors, and the demand of Torah that in Jewish territory there be one and the same law for both Jew and non-Jew. Likely following procedure, R. Yoḥanan arrested mixed-ethnicity same-sex couples and held them in custody for adjudication before Philip the Tetrarch, in whose jurisdiction the arrests had been made. Philip affirmed that R. Yoḥanan had legitimate authority over Jews, but also affirmed that the rabbi's authority did not extend over non-Jews. Accordingly, Philip allowed R. Yoḥanan to seize for execution the Jewish transgressor from each couple, but not the non-Jew.

Unlike his brothers, Philip's territory was not majority Jewish. As ruler of a multi-ethnic, multi-tribal region, Philip's domestic peace-keeping policy was continued respect for self-government. Yoḥanan b. Zakkai accepted Philip's landmark ruling. Ethnic tensions are ubiquitous throughout history, and first-century Palestine is no exception. Everyone in Philip's domain would have been paying close attention, anticipating Philip's handling of this challenge to ethnic autonomy, from Jewish fishermen to Bedouin herders, pagan priests to tribal chiefs.

Canonical Luke records the Jesus mention of four gays and lesbians. He refers to a series of incidents in which same-sex couples were targeted by authorities. In at least two cases one member of each pair was taken into custody and the other released. In other situations, involving other targets, deception was employed to effect capture. Today, law enforcement calls the first event a *raid*, a standard technique. The second event goes by two names; it is called a *sting operation* by law enforcement, and *entrapment*[98] by defense attorneys. We find this difference in perspective in the Talmud and the gospels, with the Talmud representing the point of view of law enforcement, and the gospels containing evidence from the targets.

Newspaper Style

Who

Jewish law enforcement (Pharisees headed by Yoḥanan b. Zakkai) targeted an unknown number of gay and lesbian couples. Targets would have included Jewish couples under the jurisdiction of Torah, but it was couples of mixed ethnicities which required Philip's intervention.

What

Pharisees seized gay and lesbian couples, detaining those arrested for trial, unless summary judgment was successfully pushed through. After adjudication lasting an unknown time, Philip required the release of non-Jewish prisoners.

Where

The raids were in and around the Galilean cities of Bethsaida and Chorazin, with stings and entrapments occurring in places such as fields, inner rooms in homes, etc.

When

The raids and stings occurred when enough evidence and testimony was collected. Some controversial raids, successfully defended, occurred the night.

Why

Presumably with the assistance of Jewish informants (e.g., family members), in order to purify the region of "the sin of the Gentiles" (sodomy) and the lawlessness of local Jews, as well as establish precedent in Bethsaida, Pharisees targeted gay and lesbian couples, including (perhaps especially) couples of mixed ethnicities.

How

Identifying offenders was relatively simple, obtaining convictions in the assemblies was likely easy, and the anti-gentile, pro-Torah message was clear. Where possible, Pharisees enlisted the cooperation of relatives to apprehend individuals who had brought shame on the family. A person's "perverted" sexual preference together with the choice of a gentile partner were the likely motivation for family cooperation. Using a combination of enticement and deception, Pharisees were when necessary able to lure targets to preselected locations for capture and arrest.

Background

These regional raids and stings had likely been a standard law enforcement strategy since the Hasmonean dynasty established an independent Jewish state and extended its rule over the Galilee. This Pharisee "vice squad" activity was later hampered during the Herodian dynasty under Roman jurisdiction.

Familiar Scripture in a New Context

"Shame*ful* [on you] Pharisees! for you love the front seats in the assemblies and greetings in the marketplaces. Shame*ful* [on you]! for you are like graves, outwardly beautiful, but full of pollution inside." (Luke 11:44)

"When they bring you before the assemblies of the people, don't worry about what you are to say. When the time comes, the holy spirit will teach you what to say." (Luke 12:11)

"So if anyone tells you, 'There he is out in the wilderness,' do not go out; or, 'Here he is, in the inner rooms,' do not believe it." (Matt. 24:26)

"And they shall say to you, 'See here'; or, 'see there': go not after *them*, nor follow *them*. (Luke 17:23)

"I tell you, in that night, there shall be two men in one bed; the one shall be taken, and the other shall be left. Two women shall be grinding together; the one shall be taken, and the other left." (Luke 17:34-35)

Gospel evidence for the location of the Galilee Episode is limited to the towns of Bethsaida and Chorazin. The present thesis argues that these two cities were the location of R. Yoḥanan's policy-testing, precedent-setting conflict with Philip. With their large

Jewish populations, the tetrarchies of Archelaus and Antipas would not have precipitated conflict quite like this one between the Jewish and Roman judicial systems, although similar situations could have arisen in Sepphoris and Tiberias. The Jews would have had considerably less clout with Philip. It is possible that tactics which worked with Archelaus and Antipas in their Jewish-majority territories would not have worked as well with Philip. The Jews were demographically so small they were not even mentioned in the summary descriptions of Philip's domain in Luke and Josephus.

Philip's General Situation

Philip was in a very fortunate situation. First, he governed during a period of relative peace between the two empires, Roman and Parthian. Second, his father Herod the Great had taken action to ensure greater safety on a major highway through his territory, the road from Damascus to Jerusalem. Third, the peace of his administration, and his apparent governing style suggest that Philip himself had uniquely adaptive leadership qualities. His peaceable and adaptive governing style are attested by the absence of salacious stories of atrocities and blunders such as those of Herod the Great and Herod Archelaus, and by the comparative silence surrounding his 38-year tenure as tetrarch.

Some geopolitical background is necessary to understand Philip's context and the situation between the two superpowers, the Parthian empire and the Roman republic. Their first conflict took place in 54-53 BCE, when an ill-advised and unauthorized Roman invasion (by Crassus) suffered a humiliating defeat at the hands of the Parthians, who then successfully conquered Syria. Syria borders the Palestine region in the north. Julius Caesar's plan to retaliate against Parthia was interrupted in 44 BCE when senators assassinated him. Two years after the assassination, Roman leaders successfully fought Caesar's assassins and their Parthian allies. This victory returned much of the Middle East to Roman hegemony. For the next several generations each empire respected the territory of the other and initiated no offensives.

The next major conflict between the two empires was in the early second century CE, nearly a century after the events of the Galilee Episode. Thus, Philip's rule was in the middle of a century-and-a-half period of healthy respect between Rome and Parthia. This was the peaceful geopolitical situation when Philip inherited the northernmost territory of his father. He was 27.

Rome had declared his father Herod king of Israel in 34 BCE, but he had to defeat the Parthian-backed regime in order to take possession of his throne. In effect the Romans said to him, "If you can take the territory, it's yours with our blessing." It took three years, and he reigned a little over thirty. In his will Herod said he wanted his dominion was to remain intact under his son Archelaus, but Rome said "No" and established a tetrarchy with three of Herod's sons (Archelaus, Antipas and Philip) and his sister (Salome I) as rulers.

Herod's son Philip was born in 26 BCE, about eight years into his father's reign. While we don't have much of a record of Philip's actions, we know what was going on around him. He was a toddler when his father, from his own resources, provided his subjects with food during a famine. From age six to twelve his father was supervising the construction of the spectacular city and port of Caesarea Maritima. Then Philip experienced a change of scenery. From the age of twelve Philip spent his adolescence in Rome receiving the education in history, philosophy and religion appropriate for a future ruler in the empire. Historians do us a disservice when they caricature such education as hostage taking. Philip was educated in the religion of the pantheon, the philosophy of the Greeks, the politics of the Romans, and the mores of the ruling class. He was two years into his education when his father began rebuilding the Jerusalem temple.

When Philip was 19 years old his aging father executed two of Philip's half-brothers for conspiring against him. Three years later the king executed another half-brother for similar reasons. That same year (4 BCE), King Herod executed over 40 militant Jews in Jerusalem in the Gold Eagle Incident. Philip was 22.

It is important to know what was expected of Philip when his father died and he was appointed tetrarch of Batanea, Iturea and Trachonitis. Rome tasked all its client rulers with two major priorities: tax collection and policing the roads. Banditry was especially bad in Philip's region of Trachonitis.

Philip's father had already worked on this. He had needed to safeguard merchants, travelers and religious tourists traveling from Damascus to Jerusalem. To do this, and to populate the region, in 9 BCE Herod offered a Jewish Idumean general from Babylon an incentive. If he would settle his people, some 500 horse archers and their families (totaling some 3,000) on the border of Trachonitis ("lava land") and patrol the main road, Herod would allow them to establish a settlement with no tribute, fees or taxes. As a result, the thriving city of Bathyra was established. The notorious king had taken necessary steps to bring peace and prosperity to the region about half a decade before his death.

Shortly before his death in 4 BCE, King Herod placed that Gold Eagle above the temple gate. In response, the king burned to death the two Pharisees, Judas and Matthias, with the 40 militants. This unmanageability and violence may have influenced Rome's decision to divide the kingdom in four, which was probably contemplated as an option prior to his death.

Herod was about seventy years old.

His sister Salome I received the smallest territory, a southern coastal area that included Yavneh, the future refuge of Jews loyal to Rome. His son Antipas ruled Galilee while Archelaus ruled the larger areas of Samaria, Judea and Idumea.

Philip's domain were mainly clans of the typical nomadic-sedentary Arab mix. It included two desolate lava-flow areas (e.g., Trachonitis) and more fertile areas such as Gaulanitis (modern-day Golan). In addition to the territories officially under his jurisdiction according to Josephus and the gospels, the individually autonomous Greek cities of the Decapolis would have been in his sphere of influence.

Some information about the Decapolis is necessary to picture the geography of Philip's political situation. The Decapolis refers to ten "Greek" cities which stretched from Damascus in the north to Philadelphia in the south[99], a distance of some 109 miles. The history of the Decapolis extends from the first century BCE to the first century CE, although the histories of individual cities go back considerably. Gadara, known from the gospels for pigs and demons, was one of the central cities of the Decapolis. In other eras, Gadara was the birthplace of important Cynic writers, including Menippus of Gadara (300 BCE) and Oenomaus of Gadara (2nd cent. CE).

Philip selected Banias to be his capital, renaming it Caesarea Philippi. Banias was the western edge of his territory around the temple of Pan. It had one especially beautiful pool and a large cave which probably inspired the original nature and fertility cult, one of the high places of the Old Testament. Over the years the capital Caesarea Philippi contained numerous temples, including sites for Zeus, Hermes, Nemesis, Echo and Tyche, as well as some Nymphs. The chief temple was devoted to the half-goat, half-man deity Pan, the god of wild nature. Thus, Caesarea Philippi was a center of Roman religion and emperor worship. Each worship center would have had area for both priests and support staff.

Philip was well-aware of the stakes of his position. In his early life as a son of Herod and during his education in Rome he would have learned of the humiliating defeat of Crassus and his greed-motivated invasion of Parthia. He had seen three half-brothers executed for conspiracy by his ailing father. His half-brother Archelaus governed Samaria, Judea and Idumea for ten years before Rome ordered him into exile for misrule.

Of all Herod the Great's offspring, Philip seems to have profited most from his Roman education. I believe Philip's temperament and experience were reinforced by the Stoicism he would have learned in Rome. Stoicism is a sober and moderate philosophy of life. We can call Philip a Stoic the way we might call a king a Humanist or a prime minister a Pragmatist. Josephus doesn't use the word Stoic, but he does emphasize stoic qualities in the tetrarch's character sketch. Josephus wrote that Philip was moderate and quiet in his personal life and governance. Josephus records that he dwelt among his people continually (many believe he traveled in the style of a Bedouin sheikh), with a small group of advisors and friends, stopping to hear complaints personally and render justice immediately. That he spent his entire 38-year tenure traveling his domain is not necessary to know that he circulated among his people enough to earn the reputation Josephus reports.

Two central Stoic virtues, moderation and justice, are highlighted by Josephus for the benefit of his Roman readers. The two other central virtues, wisdom and courage, are easily inferred from his account. Philip's domain was roughly twice the size of Galilee. There is no better way for a leader to know his people and be known by them, to govern effectively, than to travel and live among them. That is wisdom. The fourth Stoic virtue, courage, is seen in 1) persevering in the "strategy" of dwelling among his subjects 2) for a long period of time, 3) trusting much for his safety in the strength of tribal loyalties, 4) possibly in the face of skeptical family members who 5) were likely incredulous at Philip "going native".

If this book's general thesis is correct, and Luke 17: 34-35 refers to mixed ethnicity gay and lesbian couples, then the judicial outcome described in these verses is completely consistent with Philip's situation. Allowing Pharisees to govern Jews according to their own laws and traditions was consistent with Roman policy. Refusing to allow Pharisees to impose their laws and traditions on other ethnicities, on non-Jews, would continue Roman respect for the integrity and independence of all ethnic groups, including the Jews.

Philip exercised Stoic wisdom in terms of good sense. He exercised justice in terms of equity and fair dealing. His overall strategy was to tabernacle among his people, rendering justice upon arrival at any location. This displayed courage, requiring endurance of difficult travel, confidence in his purpose and technique, and sheer hard work. Finally, Stoic moderation was evident in the propriety of adopting local (Bedouin) forms of justice, and the modesty of refusing the creature comforts of a palace. In a geopolitical framework, Philip's governing style ensured that if the Parthians had any interest in meddling and undermining Roman hegemony, there would have been no foothold for the devil.

It is quite appropriate to compare the Galilee episode with other incidents of tension between Roman and Jewish officials. If we look at some of Josephus' Pharisee episodes and compare them to the incident in Luke 17:34-35, the stories in Josephus are quite lurid. The Luke 17 episode is quite orderly and by-the-book. When the two couples are apprehended by Jewish law enforcement, there is no immediate stoning of all the parties, no "extrajudicial execution" of the gentile offenders.

Indeed, the two incidents are so orderly that they seem to illustrate the procedural situation *after* a judicial decision had been made. In other words, they might represent settled law. If we were discussing *Miranda v. Arizona*, we might discuss the initial 1963 arrest and trial, the Supreme Court case, or the subsequent restraint of law enforcement.

Using this sequence, Luke 17 would not refer to the Pharisaic arrest and conviction, or to the legal reasoning behind Philip's decision, but to a situation when the legal conflict had subsided. After the 1966 Supreme Court decision, you will read the suspect his rights. After Philip's ruling, one will be seized, the other left.

If we look at the story of R. Yoḥanan explaining Torah to Antigonus the Hegemon (Philip the Tetrarch) using the same grid, the Talmudic exchange reflects some portion of a trial, where Yoḥanan b. Zakkai is the prosecutor and Philip is the judge.

We know Philip was born in 26 BCE, making him 56 years old when Bethsaida-Julius was founded in 30 CE. It is more difficult to calculate the age of Yoḥanan b. Zakkai. His birth year is variously estimated to be 30 BCE, 15 BCE and 1 CE. Such uncertainty is not uncommon for ancient figures. R. Yoḥanan was between 30 and 60 when his contemporary Philip issued the commemorative coin in 30 CE. When he prosecuted his case before Philip, he was between 30 and 60 years old.

We have already discussed the Talmudic exchange between Ribaz and Antigonus (the real-life Yoḥanan b. Zakkai and Philip the Tetrarch) which demonstrated the unwillingness of the Talmud authorship to record a positive example of accountability to non-Jews, which resulted in this "exchange" devoid of historical context. The inferred context of the original incident shows that R. Yoḥanan was willing to make pragmatic compromises with Rome. The Jews survived because of his compromises, but many of them despised him for it. Centuries later he was viewed negatively, and he was none too popular in his own day, if his ouster from Yavneh is any indicator.

What he established at Yavneh has been characterized as a yeshiva of sorts, a Torah school, but was a kind of "government in exile" from Jerusalem after the destruction of the Temple state.

Ribaz ruled by fiat, and by his "executive orders" mandated many changes necessary for Israel to transition from a nation to a religion, from being building-centered to book-centered. For his troubles he was unceremoniously removed from leadership under murky circumstances. This sort of murkiness generally results from the awkward and embarrassing actions required of the winners in unprecedented circumstances.

Two pictures of Ribaz emerge from the Talmud. One picture outlined in chapter two is an arbitrary and capricious decision-maker guided only by his sense of the situation. The other is of a man who compromises with the enemy, a collaborator. This willingness to make fruitful compromises when necessary means that in Jewish circles the tradition of Ribaz remains controversial.

If the present thesis is correct, and Luke 17:34-35 refers to gay and lesbian couples facing legal sanctions, then both parts of this picture of Ribaz are reinforced. The Pharisee has resisted Roman hegemony and pressed for official recognition of Temple-state jurisdiction over non-Jews. Before 30 CE, Bethsaida was like any other Jewish town. After 30 CE, it was a *Roman* city. He resisted Roman hegemony but he played by the rules. He recognized Roman hegemony at some point, which is seen in the fact that he and the tetrarch eventually worked out an arrangement.

There is a contrast between lurid headline events and civilized process events. The Gold Eagle conflict some 34 years earlier is one of the lurid events. In that conflict Herod the Great had deliberately flaunted his disregard for Jewish sensibilities, and Pharisees responded with equal disregard for Roman sensibilities. It was by no means a fair fight. The coercive forces of Herod were stronger than the forces of the Pharisees.

The Galilee Episode was a civilized process event. The police procedural description in Luke 17 is, if you can get past capital punishment for consensual behavior between adults, in the latter category, a civilized process. Admittedly, working in the north,

Ribaz didn't face the degree of tension and provocation characteristic of the Gold Eagle incident. Mattathias and Judas reacted to a deliberate provocation. In contrast, Ribaz had a test case with the wisest, least confrontational son of Herod.

Given the greater Jewish population leverage in the south, it seems possible that Exodus 12:49[100] might have carried more weight there than in the largely Bedouin territory of Philip. Canonical Exodus requires that Jews and non-Jews to be subject to the same Law in Torah territory: "One law shall be to him that is homeborn, and unto the stranger that sojourneth among you" (Ex. 12:49). Ribaz may have hoped that by invoking this particular law and citing some Judean precedents of Jewish sovereignty over resident gentiles, Philip might allow him to execute gentiles for engaging in forbidden sexual activities with Jews.

If Philip had relented, granting Ribaz jurisdiction over certain gentile sexual offenders, three things would have been materially altered. First, it might have changed the career path of Ribaz, which included his time in Jerusalem during the siege and the pivotal historical moment in Yavneh. Second, the story of Ribaz and Antigonus might be radically different. Third, the New Testament would read differently, if it even existed. But this is speculation.

Clearly, chopping away at a Gold Eagle was more militant than working through established legal channels to clarify a point of law or enforcement procedure. For the present thesis to work, then a willingness on R. Yoḥanan's part to work vigorously and by the rules is necessary. This assumes diligence, that he rarely missed an opportunity to further Temple-state interests during the occupation.

Evidence for Incident,
Episode, *and* Campaign

Many people agree that some sort of persecution occurred in the early church, and most also agree that the synoptic gospels contain evidence of persecution. However, there seems to be a problem in the timeline. Evidence of persecution exists in the gospels, but "Christians" were not yet differentiated from Jews. Decades ago, before my son came out, before I found the homosexuals in Luke 17, I had been curious about persecution in the gospels. What was this persecution about? It occurred before the account of Jesus' crucifixion and resurrection, well before Paul's conversion.

I am focusing on a single episode, the meaning of two verses. I debated within myself whether to characterize these events as an incident, an episode or a campaign. I settled on *episode* for two reasons. First, because in Q there is evidence of two raids, one on two men in a field, and one on two women grinding together. The idea of a single incident is simply incorrect. Second, this evidence suggests a legal decision which resulted from these raids. Archaeological evidence[101] does exist which supports the probability of a sustained campaign, and there is New Testament evidence of a campaign perceived as persecution. The evidence for those events is in the earliest layer of gospel tradition.[102] But in this book, evidence of a campaign is presented to provide context. The present thesis concerns the events preserved in two verses.

It is generally agreed that the split between Jews and Christians did not occur immediately. Jesus was a Jew and his people were Jews. Any action against this group was a domestic matter. Q scholars have asked why no independent Q source was preserved and believe that a supporting community ceased to exist. The disappearance of the Q Community was a Jewish phenomenon, and is explained, not by a single incident or episode, but by a prolonged Pharisaic campaign to Clean Up the Galilee, to cleanse it of the unclean gentile presence. During this lengthy campaign, numismatic evidence suggests that trade in Upper Galilee between some Jewish towns with non-Jewish communities dwindled to zero.

There is archaeological evidence in Galilee for such a campaign. First is the gradual disappearance of ESA pottery. ESA is Phoenician Eastern Sigillata A, an imported red dishware used by the well-to-do.[103] Second is the gradual appearance of Jewish ritual baths called *mikvot* (sing. *mikveh*) in what archaeologists believe were private homes and refuge caves. Finally, numismatic evidence suggests a change in trade patterns.

Coin hoards in Galilee range from mainly gentile coins to hoards of mixed gentile and Hasmonean coins to completely Hasmonean caches. These hoards suggest that many Galilean towns had virtually no non-Jewish coinage, suggesting the absence of commercial trade with gentile economies such as Phoenicia and the Decapolis. Governments attempt to influence commercial trade because it is a source of tax revenue. Intercourse of any kind with gentiles—sexual, social or commercial—was defiling according to Pharisees. Even if Jesus followers were not the rabbi's primary target, any incipient Q community disappeared because of the imposition of Judean law and order on the Galilee. This was first the policy of the Hasmonean dynasty, the first independent Jewish dynasty over Israel for centuries, and next the policy of the Pharisees, many of whom were tax collection agents and law enforcement for the Judean Temple state.

Regarding the applicability of the words *episode* and *campaign*. Both words apply, but to different locales. What transpired in the Galilee of Antipas (which is what we think of when we consider Galilee) was a campaign, which also eliminated or drove out the earliest Jesus followers. What transpired in the tetrarchy of Philip was probably much briefer, an episode. If the present thesis is correct, the episode centered in Bethsaida may be better documented than the campaign in Galilee proper because Philip effectively limited Yoḥanan b. Zakkai's Torah efforts in a single, quite public stroke.

Pharisees, led at least in part by Yoḥanan b. Zakkai, waged a decades-long campaign to bring Galilee under Torah. This was consistent with the Pharisaic policy of exerting Torah authority over every level of government possible. This chapter is concerned with evidence for one episode, a series of incidents, centered in Bethsaida and Chorazin. These incidents involved Torah enforcement raids in the wee hours of the morning targeting gay and lesbian couples, and entrapments involving deception and enticement to prearranged locations.

Sting Operations

As we strive for clarity, definitions are important when we use contemporary terms to discuss antiquity. Stratfor Enterprises posted the following website description of sting operations.[104]

> Because sting operations cover a wide variety of crimes and use different techniques depending on the operation's immediate or long-term purpose, it is difficult to define precisely what a sting operation is. However, with some exceptions, all sting operations contain four basic elements
>
> 1. an opportunity or enticement to commit a crime, either created or exploited by police;
>
> 2. a targeted likely offender or group of offenders for a particular crime type;
>
> 3. an undercover or hidden police officer or surrogate, or some form of deception; and
>
> 4. a "gotcha" climax when the operation ends with arrests.[105]

Elsewhere, the Stratfor Enterprises police manual reads, "The involvement of a legal professional ensures that the operation is conducted lawfully and avoids entrapment while guaranteeing that the criteria required to successfully take the case to trial are met." [106] First century Jewish lawyers, or scribes, are mentioned three times in the earliest layers of gospel tradition (Q2 and Q34). The scribes in the gospels are what the Stratfor manual calls "legal professionals."

In the gospels, we must examine two clusters of material dealing with stings and raids. The first is the much-discussed material in Luke 11 and 12, the second is in Luke 17. How this information got separated is beyond the scope of this study. It is enough to be aware that this material is in the early layers of the gospel tradition, conveniently labeled the Q source.

In their canonical incarnation the clusters are in highly developed sections. Recasting a section that describes a past action so that it becomes a prediction is fairly easy, simply change the verb tense from past to future. Certain prophetic, predictive sections of Luke 11, 12 and 17 describe events that had already occurred. According to some, this prophecy-had-already-happened element would make this a preterist approach,[107] although I do not consider myself a preterist.

Warnings about Entrapment

The "inner rooms" were places of seclusion and privacy in a home, where under normal circumstances intimate conversations and activities could safely occur. We use virtually identical privacy language when we talk about "what goes on behind closed doors" and "what happens in the bedroom." The usage in the Tosefta Sanhedrin is paralleled in the gospels, in the context of warnings.

> Be on your guard against the yeast of the Pharisees, which is hypocrisy.

> There is nothing concealed that will not be disclosed, or
> hidden that will not be made known.
> What you have said in the dark will be heard in the daylight,
> and what you have whispered in the ear in the *inner rooms* will
> be proclaimed from the roofs. (Luke 12:1-3)

The seemingly minor editing and expansion to Luke 12:1 was
enough to deflect our attention away from a concrete situation, and
toward a general moral failing. The cause of concern is changed
from flesh-and-blood adversaries to an internal moral failing.
When we detect the new focus, the verse's valuable but secondary
moralizing is diminished in importance and the warning of verse 1
is simple, "Beware of the Pharisees."

In canonical Matthew we are being warned about a "false
messiah," but the Matthean scribes changed the subject. In the
older strata of tradition, we were being warned about entrapment.
Today, if the authorities see you as a threat or a convenient target,
they are authorized to use deception to solicit incriminating
testimony. The police will lie.

> So if anyone tells you, "There he is out in the wilderness,"
> do not go out; or, "Here he is, in the inner rooms," do not believe
> it. (Matt. 24:26)

In both the Jewish Talmud and the Christian gospels, the inner
rooms are the setting for privacy and secrecy. The gospels warn
you against thinking your privacy is safe, and the Talmud instructs
law enforcement how to observe and apprehend people who
privately violate Torah. The Tosefta Sanhedrin is written from the
Torah enforcement perspective and provides a checklist to ensure
the testimony of the Sages will meet legal demands and survive
cross examination. First, you place yourself where you cannot be
seen. Second, you make sure you can clearly see the target.
Third, be sure you can clearly hear the target. In another century,
all you have to do is insert a microphone into the scene, a reel-to-

reel tape recorder in an adjoining room, and a guy with head phones.

Matthew and Luke represent the point of view of the targets, warning people about specific entrapment techniques.

Matthew warns, "Do not to believe what they tell you" (Matt. 24:26). Luke says in effect, "Anything you say can and will be used against you" (Luke 12:1-3). Any expectation of privacy you may have is an illusion. Some people must be coached to be suspicious. "If they're after you, they will be prepared. Success isn't measured in the number of cases lost, you know."

Anatomy of a Sting Operation

#1 Identify Potential Target

#2 Evaluate if they Pose a Potential Threat

#3 & 4 Open Official Case

　　　　　Make Contact

#5 Let Informant Incriminate Themselves

#6 Make an Arrest

Information from Stratfor Enterprises, LLC. "Anatomy of a Sting Operation." April 16, 2015. https://worldview.stratfor.com/article/anatomy-sting-operation.

Defendant Trial Preparation:
Luke 11:39 to 12:12

This passage of Luke's gospel, in an earlier form, was a warning about the Pharisees. As legal *pre-arrest preparation,* the section encapsulated the lessons learned from an actual campaign that Galilean Jews had already suffered. The first section (QS34) is the most developed, expanded to include a total of six "shame on you" statements directed at both Pharisees and lawyers, and expanded again to include the "this generation" paragraph. After an initial mention of official Pharisaic duties, it is more ethically developed than the subsequent couplets. The following three couplets warn people that they have no expectation of privacy, minimize the nearly certain death penalty they face, and suggest that mounting a defense against the charges was neither pertinent nor realistic.

The two sides of this legal situation are represented by two sets of documents. The first warning that Jesus' audience read was simple: "Beware of the Pharisees" (Luke 12:1). These are the targets talking, the perps, which might mean they are accomplices before and after the fact, fellow conspirators. Later scribes massaged this warning in an ethical direction, adding *the leaven of* and *which is hypocrisy.*

The second set of documents is the Talmud, which says a sound entrapment procedure involved sending two Sages to witness the target's self-incrimination.[108] That is law enforcement talking, the cops.

Pre-arrest warnings are in a section designated as QS34 through QS37 by Q specialists. QS34 mentions Pharisees in one of their official capacities. In North America many people aren't used to thinking of religious offerings as a tax, but Matthew 17:24 (a canonical enhancement of Q) reminds us of the Christ's willing acceptance of the tax burden to support the Temple state. Luke 11:42a reminds us of one of the many official functions of Pharisees: government tax collection. Publicans were Jews who collected taxes for Rome, and many Pharisees were Jews who collected taxes for the Jerusalem hierarchy. [109]

> Shame*ful* [on you] Pharisees! for you are scrupulous about giving a tithe of mint and dill and cumin to the priests, but you neglect justice and the love of God.

Luke 11:42 portrays Jesus castigating Pharisees for focusing on revenue enhancement instead of justice and love. Throughout QS34 Pharisees are pictured as high-status, privileged officials, and as Christians themselves became more hierarchical and respectable, the value of Pharisees-as-Bad-Guys evolved away from Torah *enforcers* toward a more ethical and moral "examples of bad leadership." Not recognizing Pharisees as law enforcement was more appealing as Christian scribes found new and valuable uses for Pharisees in the Luke 11 expansion pack (vv 39-53[110]).

Moving to QS35, Luke 12:2 could be untouched from its original use as a pre-arrest warning. "Nothing is hidden that will not be made known, or secret that will not come to light." We would say, "When they bust you, the cops will know everything." QS36 has been used throughout church history to encourage communities facing deadly persecution.

> Don't be afraid of those who can kill the body, but can't kill the soul. Rather fear the one who is able to destroy both body and soul in Gehenna (hell fire) Can't you buy five sparrows for two cents? Not one of them will fall to the ground without God knowing about it. Even the hairs of your head are all numbered. So don't be afraid. You are worth more than many sparrows.

QS37 has likewise been used to exhort Jesus followers to be faithful witnesses. "Every one who admits in public that they know me, the son of man will acknowledge before the angels of God. But the one who disowns me in public, the son of man will disown before the angels of God. Whoever makes a speech against the son of man will be forgiven. But whoever speaks against the holy spirit will not be forgiven. When they bring you before the assemblies of the people, don't worry about what you are to say. When the time comes, the holy spirit will teach you what to say."

None of the immediately preceding discussion of Luke is new or remarkable. What is new is the realization that the persecution Jesus witnessed included nonobservant gay and lesbian Jews. This lends new significance to Saul the Pharisee's comment, "they which commit such things are worthy of death" (Rom. 1). He wrote those words as a former Torah enforcement official who arrested criminals and supervised their execution. As a trusted law enforcement official, Saul would have legitimately targeted nonobservant gay and lesbian Jews. **It was his job.**

Legal warnings and coaching are common today. Esurance recommends that if you are in a traffic accident you should "avoid admitting fault or blaming others while at the scene."[111] The Washington Peace Center publishes an article titled "FAQs About Risking Arrest at the Capitol."[112] The activist organization Act-Up has an online resource titled "Civil Disobedience Training - Act Up."[113] When a group anticipates arrests of its members, giving the members advice on what to expect is only reasonable. The advice is based on experience and the anticipated continuation of struggle. This suggests that whoever wrote these warnings knew what had happened in the past and expected further conflict.

Luke 12:11-12 are realistic advice for activists whose fate is predetermined. "This is movement work, not petty crime. You are not getting off for this, you don't want to, and you don't need to. You have two concerns: the truth, and what others will do who follow you." Therefore,

> When they bring you before the assemblies,
> do not be anxious how or what you are to say;
>
> For the Holy Spirit will teach you in that hour
> what you are to say.

In other words, "Religious leaders have put us on trial in the assembly before, and they'll do it again. Don't be surprised when they come prepared to prosecute their case; they will know everything. They have already rehearsed their witnesses. Don't worry about getting off, you're already convicted and dead. They will live with what you say when this party is over. You won't be around to see how things play out."

This trial preparation is wisdom based on defendant experiences in synagogue trials conducted by the Pharisees. Decades later, Christian scribes elaborated on various elements of the story, in order to make it more devotional, more relevant to readers for whom the threat of arrest was over, when death penalty trials overseen by Pharisees in the local assemblies (synagogues) were a distant

> **First-Century Galilee Sting Warnings**
> - **Beware of the Pharisees** (Luke 12:1)
> - **Beware: Legal Inequality** (Luke 17:34-35)
> - **Beware of Entrapment** (Luke 17:23; Matt 24:26)
> - **Beware the Inner Room** (Luke 12:3; Matt 24:26)
> - **Beware: No Expectation of Privacy** (Luke 12:2-3)
> - **Beware: Do Not Believe Them** (Luke 17:23; Matt 24:26)
>
> © 2018, Ronald Goetz

memory. "Ironically," some of the most fruitful material for devotional and homiletical expansion was the material on the Pharisees, which had become the *leaven* of the Pharisees. The practical warning about Pharisees as opponents, as legal prosecutors, evolved into moral and ethical warnings about becoming *like* Pharisees.

Q's Big Picture: This Generation

Pharisees are specifically mentioned in Luke 12:39-52, but these agents are sometimes left unnamed and their presence inferred. One instance of such implicit presence in Q occurs in Luke 11:49-50, which presumably refers to actual people killed and

> Scribes and Pharisees are parallel to District Attorneys and the Police, even more to the DOJ and the FBI.

persecuted.

> Therefore also the Wisdom said, I will send them prophets and apostles, and some of them they will kill and persecute, so that the blood of all the prophets which has been shed from the foundation of the world may be required from this generation.

"They will kill and persecute." One of the instruments of organized power is its legal system. The nebulous "they" in verse 49 includes these agents of law enforcement, the Pharisees. This couplet reminds potential defendants of their place in this drama. They are arrest targets intended for execution.

Law Enforcement Knows More Than You Expect

Your opponents are engaged in information gathering and investigation. That's their job. They are building a case against you. What they know will astonish you.

> Nothing is covered which will not be revealed and hidden which will not be made known. (Q 12:2)

> What I tell you in the darkness speak in the light, and what you hear as a whisper in your ear, proclaim upon the housetops. (Q 12:3)

Your arrest and trial only come when authorities are confident of their case against you.

The Worst they Can Do (Luke 12:4-5)

Your activist leaders will tell you: "*They* live to serve civil order; *you* live to serve the divine. You live for ultimate values, ultimate meaning. The worst they can do is kill you."

> And do not fear those who kill the body but are not able to kill the soul. Fear, rather the one who is able to kill both in Gehenna.

Today we might say, "*Your* future differs from theirs. *You* have a higher calling."

Misunderstanding Scribes and Pharisees

We have generally misunderstood the pre-70 social role of scribes and Pharisees. It is widely acknowledged in our English and Christian translations that the scribes were lawyers. The ESV subhead at Luke 11:37 is "Warnings to the Pharisees and Lawyers." And we know that the Pharisees focused on greater adherence to Torah. But the experience of a religion-based state is so foreign to us that we miss the role of the scribes

> ### Luke 11:39 to 12:12
> ### Pharisee Warning Summary
> - Do not trust the Pharisees. Their rules and goals differ from yours.
> - Nothing is hidden from them. When the Pharisees arrest you, they will have sufficient evidence to convict.
> - Do not fear those who can only kill your body. You are precious to God.
> - Nothing will save you at trial. When needed, the spirit of God will let you know what to say to the people who are prosecuting and sentencing you.
>
> © 2018, Ronald Goetz

and Pharisees as lawyers and law enforcement. What we see is the close coordination of district attorneys and the police, vis-à-vis *Law and Order*. I will not be treating this asso-ciation as a focus in this book, but it is a major back-ground factor. I used to think scribes and Pharis-ees were parallel to theologians and pastors in con-temporary terms. This is not the case. Scribes and Pharisees are parallel to District Attorneys and the Police, even more to the DOJ and the FBI. We consistently see them acting as Torah enforcement. In the gospels we rarely if ever see them in teaching roles, except in the sense that the police teach values when they make arrests.

The Pharisees have an even closer parallel today.[114] We find groups similar to the Pharisees in the Morality Police in certain Islamic countries. In Iran they are called *Gasht-e Ershad*.[115] Saudi Arabia has the Committee for the Promotion of Virtue and the Prevention of Vice, or the *Mutawa* (which means "Particularly Obedient").[116] Sudan has the Public Order Police, who have been able to order immediate trials where sentences range from flogging to imprisonment.[117]

In the past I found Pharisaic pickiness and their reputed popularity a bit baffling. Such cognitive dissonance is diminished, now that I understand that Pharisees were popular for the same reason the police are popular today. The Pharisees were not popular as clergymen, they were popular as law enforcement. It must be remembered that Pharisees have a history. As the fortunes of Israel changed, so did the role of Torah enforcement. The original Torah focus of individual Pharisees remained constant despite the destruction of the Temple state. That was perhaps the critical element of continuity.

Remember, as the Roman empire crumbled, the Roman Catholic Church provided stability for Europe. The need for order remained constant. Ivan Zybin of the Okhrana—the Tsarist secret police—found a place in the Cheka—the Soviet secret police. The need for domestic intelligence remained constant. The Zion Mule Corps and the Jewish Legion were units in the British Army before they became the foundation of Haganah. The need for skilled and disciplined personnel remained constant. When he migrated to America after the war, Werner von Braun worked at NASA. Demand for temperament and expertise is an institutional constant.

In Palestine, the role of the Pharisees underwent a stark change when the Temple state collapsed. Similarly, the literary and religious function of Pharisees-as-Bad-Guys in Luke 11:39 to 12:12 evolved. The devotional and homiletical use of the *leaven* of the Pharisees was certainly valuable. Today, the bad things Christians associate with "being a Pharisee," the scrupulosity, the hypocrisy, the self-serving, should be avoided. But by the time the Q document came into the hands of Matthean and Lukan scribes, "Pharisees" were already evolving from one genre of antagonist to another. They were already in literary transition from bad cops to bad ministers.

Think how different the history of Christendom might have been if a straight up account of these trials had been preserved without the accreted ground clutter. Think of church history with fewer inquisitions, fewer excommunications, fewer manuals of *discipline*. But the demands, even the legitimate demands, of organized communities will not be frustrated. The "needs" of the institution are reflected in even the earliest strata of the gospels.[118]

Jew and Gentile: Differing Legal Status

Making a political distinction between Jews and gentiles in legal status and treatment is taken for granted in some places today. It was in the Roman Empire, also. Sandra Gambetti describes in thorough and helpful detail such political and religious differentiation in her book, *The Alexandrian Riots of 38 C.E. and the Persecution of the Jews*. Gambetti describes how, when he founded Alexandria in 322 BCE, Alexander the Great relocated a large number of Jews to his new Egyptian city, who were legally granted residency in an area labeled the Delta District (Δ). Almost 300 years later, when Egypt was conquered by Rome (30 BCE), prior legal arrangements were honored, and the Jewish right to reside in the Delta District was grandfathered in. Nevertheless, this arrangement did not prevent conflict, which is the subject of Gambetti's book. Disparate treatment under the law based on religion and ethnicity appears to have been common in the first century. The Alexandrian riots of 38 CE occurred at virtually the same historical moment as the Galilee Episode.

There are at least two recognized examples of jurisdictional conflict in the New Testament. First, in the book of Acts Paul exploits of perks of dual "citizenship," who was both a Jew and a Roman citizen and was, according to the story, able to gain passage to Rome and an audience with Caesar. The second example of jurisdictional conflict is present in the canonical accounts of the trials of Jesus. In addition to these New Testament episodes, there are two contemporary controversies which closely parallel the situation described in Luke 17:34-35.

Catch and Release

On April 1, 2018, the American president tweeted, "Border Patrol Agents are not allowed to properly do their job at the Border because of ridiculous liberal (Democrat) laws like Catch & Release. Getting more dangerous. 'Caravans' coming. Republicans must go to Nuclear Option to pass tough laws NOW. NO MORE DACA DEAL!" Two months earlier the president used the phrase "catch and release" regarding Chicago.

> Chicago's slide toward criminal anarchy is a national disgrace, as even its top cop[119] seems to understand…. One major reason the perps do not fear the judicial machinery is the Illinois law enacted 9 months ago formally called the "Bail Reform Act," but widely derided as the "catch and release policy." [120]

Two years earlier, the following headline hit the internet, including the NPR news site. "California Cops Frustrated With 'Catch-And-Release' Crime-Fighting." All over the internet reports said the police were "frustrated," "fuming" and "grumbling" because of "Catch and Release."[121] The phrase came into political currency during the second Bush presidency. A first-century version of "Catch and Release" is the story behind Luke 17:34-35.

Yoḥanan b. Zakkai came into conflict with a Roman "Catch and Release" order when it came to non-Jewish sexual transgressors. At a minimum the rabbi had directed apprehensions which included two gentile homosexuals, one male and one female, and been forced to "catch and release" the gentile detainees. At some point he was in a jurisdictional struggle with a Rome-appointed ruler, most likely Philip the Tetrarch, whose territory included Bethsaida Julias.

It takes time for nations to develop the protocols and traditions necessary for smooth relations. After the collapse of the Hasmonean dynasty in 37 BCE, the legal friction between Jewish leadership and Roman leadership probably increased. The story of Yoḥanan b. Zakkai and Antigonus the Hegemon is evidence of this conflict.

Face-saving is evident from the story's beginning. Similarly, significant political events connected to the Hasmoneans (aka Maccabees) could not be totally ignored by the Talmud authorship. As an example of "misdirection," the story of Yoḥanan b. Zakkai and Antigonue the Hegemon excels.[122] The story is akin to the fictional histories of Hanukah, which commemorated the victory of the Hasmoneans over the Seleucids, and of the 9th of Adar, which was a disguised version of the Siege of Jerusalem. The Talmudists were almost ahistorical, with no tradition of accuracy and precision in history writing as we practice it. Leopold von Ranke was far in the future, and Josephus was despised. The Talmud was originally a legal document, not a historical account.

Binational Same-Sex Couple Separation

The political utility of binational same-sex couples legally separated by religious ideologues is very familiar. In the U.S., until the 2013 repeal of relevant provisions of DOMA (Defense of Marriage Act), gay and lesbian couples had none of the protections afforded to heterosexual couples under Federal Law.[123] Same-sex couples were broken up, with non-citizen partners deported routinely. A commonplace in Christian circles is that Jesus used illustrations from everyday experience in his parables and stories. What we have in Luke 17:34-35 are couples split up over issues of sexuality and ethnicity, or what we would call nationality. We can now see that Luke 17 refers to the legal complexity of law-enforcement action against homosexuals. "One shall be seized, and the other left."

> **The Galilee Episode**
> **Q Apocalypse (QS60/Lk 17:23-37)**
>
> - Entrapment (23)
> - Suddenness of Raids (26-27)
> - Same-Sex Couples Targeted (34-35)
> - Speed of Philip's Intervention (24, 37)
> - Unequal Post-Arrest Treatment (34-35)
>
> © Ronald Goetz, 2019

Galilee Episode: Trial Phase

The newspaper rubric answers who, what, where, when, and why. We've begun to talk about what happened, who did it and to whom it was done. The next question to cover is where. I suggest that these raids were conducted in Bethsaida and Chorazin (Luke 10:12-13). The text says these two cities were condemned for their failure to repent.

> But I say unto you, that it shall be more tolerable in that day for Sodom, than for that city. Woe unto thee, Chorazin! woe unto

thee, Bethsaida! for if the mighty works had been done in Tyre and Sidon, which have been done in you, they had a great while ago repented, sitting in sackcloth and ashes.

While some scholars caution against emphasizing Bethsaida and Chorazin when discussing the provenance of Q's composition, something clearly happened there. They appear in one of the earliest strata of identifiable synoptic sources. This is not to say that they are the *ipsissima verba* words of Jesus. This is difficult to know. It simply means that, in someone's mind, the text which mentions Bethsaida and Chorazin warranted inclusion among the very early Jesus manuscripts. One reason to say that they are *historically* significant because they are not *traditionally* symbolic, as are cities like Jerusalem, Tyre or Babylon. Bethsaida and Chorazin do not appear in any Old Testament stories. It is reasonable to assume that some significant historical event took place there which merited their mention, the details of which are not recorded as a narrative, but somehow involved rejection of the message. Finally, the insignificant Galilean towns appear in the immediate context of Sodom. Unlike the appearance of Sodom in canonical Luke 17, which is not original to Q, the Luke 10 occurrence is found within the oldest gospel materials. Bethsaida and Chorazin are not only in Q, but many Q experts place this section in the first and oldest stratum of Q. Sodom and the cities of Bethsaida and Chorazin (the SBC cities) are linked in the early tradition. This suggests that in some ancient eyes the disturbance in the towns was connected to sexual transgression.

The scribe who wrote the *Pericope Eiusdem Sexus* (see discussion below) suggests that the events in Bethsaida and Chorazin were linked to the couples in Luke 17:34-35 vis-à-vis the mention of *Sodom*. It seems reasonable that the raids and jurisdictional dispute reflected in the Couples Material occurred in the two cities. The scribe who wrote the Sodom cycle uses *Sodom* with the same non-condemning tone found in Luke 10:12.

Bethsaida: Ripe for Conflict in 30 CE

In view of the number of groups competing for use of the Galilean fishery resources, the situation in Bethsaida bore careful watching. Josephus described Philip's improvements to Bethsaida and the population increase he engineered (*Ant*, 18.2). Numismatic evidence pinpoints the city's eventual elevation to imperial polis in 30 CE.[124] Bethsaida and Chorazin are mentioned in Matthew and Luke in a situation of singular condemnation, where deaths undoubtedly occurred. Among the obvious stakeholders in the Bethsaida urban expansion project would be 1) the master planner Philip the Tetrarch, 2) the region's chief Pharisee Yoḥanan b. Zakkai, 3) the labor of local and imported *'am ha-aretz* and 4) local fishermen. Conflict among these four interests alone would have been unavoidable.[125]

The Sea of Galilee is relatively small, measuring only 13 miles north to south and 8 miles across. Today its surface area is about 64 sq mi, compared to the larger Lake Tahoe (191 sq mi) and the smaller Loch Ness (22 sq mi). Going back to the first century CE, when you factor in the interests of gentile fishermen on the eastern coast of the Sea of Galilee and Herod Antipas' Tiberias on the west coast you have increased potential conflict exponentially. Bethsaida's urban renewal would have taken at least a decade. In that time there were undoubtedly conflicts of varying severity between various players. Think fisheries conflicts and fishing boat duels, a perennial occurrence in fishing economies. Think non-standard sexual incidents, likewise perennial.

Recapping the Case Thus Far

In Luke 17:28-35 there are three or four elements of the sexual theme: 1) the discussion of Lot and Sodom, 2) two men in one bed, 3) two women grinding together in the same place and 4) the couples activities "that night." This constitute the same-sex theme.

Regarding those elements, one of them is more directly connected with judgment than the others, *two men in one bed* referring to the prohibitions in Leviticus. There is nothing worthy of judgment in the Noah cycle. Also, nowhere is God mentioned as the agent of judgment, and nowhere is the word *judgment* used. In the gospel of Luke, the three elements of the same-sex theme are not related to God's judgment.

Regarding verses 34 and 35, the two lines are written as Hebrew-style poetry. Both lines contain definite sexual content, which is expressed subtly in order to not offend the sensibilities of innocent readers, but clearly enough to be understood by those who have ears to hear. The phrase *two men in one bed* is alone *prima facie* evidence for investigation, leading to the Hebrew word for *bed* embedded in the uncited prohibitions against male homosexuality in Exodus.

The disparate treatment between members of the two couples is rooted in a jurisdictional dispute between the Pharisee Yoḥanan b. Zakkai and Philip the Tetrarch in a zone of urban renewal and population dislocation (Bethsaida). As Rome's appointed man, Philip ruled a region that was overwhelmingly Arab but included Bethsaida in a sliver of northeast Galilee. The couples were ethnically mixed, a Jew and a non-Jew. Just as Ribaz did, Philip understood precedent, and did not allow Jewish law enforcement to exercise jurisdiction over non-Jews in his territory. Gentile Arabs were not subject to Torah. Since Philip's territory was the least Jewish of the three divisions, a policy of *Torah non-applicability to Arabs* would normally have had little downside.

Bethsaida and Chorazin were denounced by Jesus for rejecting his messengers. Coin evidence tells us the year of Bethsaida's imperial elevation, but with no similar documentation for Chorazin we are less certain of its ruler. The two cities are nevertheless within a few miles of each other. In Luke 10, Sodom is mentioned immediately before Bethsaida and Chorazin. The *Sodom* symbol flags the same-sex relevance there and in chapter 17, with the same non-condemning, nonjudgmental tone in both places. We may assume the raids in Luke 17:34-35 occurred in the cities mentioned in Luke 10:13. What Matthew utilized as warnings against false messiahs, Luke uses as law enforcement entrapment. "If they shall say unto you, Behold, he is in the desert; go not forth: behold, he is in the secret chambers; believe it not." Matthew's *pseudochristoi* do not appear in Luke. The passage's shared meaning element in Matthew and Luke is deliberate deception. In Matthew the deception regards the Christ, in Luke it regards police entrapment.

The reason for disparate treatment of the members of each couple is rooted in jurisdictional overlap between Yoḥanan b. Zakkai and Philip the Tetrarch. In the Talmud, this dispute over the execution of transgressing gentile women was the occasion of Yoḥanan b. Zakkai's legal justification to "Antigonus the Hegemon" for executing the "ox." The cities of Bethsaida and Chorazin were within the overlapping jurisdictions of the two men. Pharisees targeted mixed-ethnicity same-sex couples, creating opportune test cases to test the resolve of their Roman overlords and gain an edge in the new imperial city. Such legal wrangling probably took place in imperial cities like Sepphoris and Tiberias, and Philip resisted Jewish attempts to undermine Roman hegemony. He did not allow Torah-minded Pharisees to encroach on his jurisdiction over non-Jews in his domain. Arabs under his rule were not generally subject to Jewish law, similar to oxen.

Philip the Tetrarch According to Josephus

We know relatively little about Philip the Tetrarch. Most of the information we have is found in a brief summary of his life and rule in *Antiquities of the Jews*, chapter 18, by Josephus.

He had shown himself a person of moderation and quietness in the conduct of his life and government; he constantly lived in that country which was subject to him.

He used to travel with a few choice friends; his tribunal also, on which he sat in judgment, followed him in his travels.

And when any-one met him who wanted his assistance, he made no delay but had his tribunal set down immediately, wheresoever he happened to be, and sat down upon it, and heard his complaint;

He there ordered the guilty that were convicted to be punished, and absolved those that had been accused unjustly.... he left no sons behind him ...
Ant. 18.4.6

> Josephus said, "[Philip] there ordered the guilty that were convicted to be punished, and absolved those that had been accused unjustly" (*Antiquities* 18.4).
>
> Luke said twice, "One shall be seized, the other left" (Luke 17:34-35).

There are two elements to note here. First is the focus on his judicial presence in his territories. He maintained a traveling court which may have functioned as a final court of appeal. While this is not stated by Josephus, there was nevertheless no need for his tribal subjects in Batanea or Trachonitis to journey hundreds of miles to Caesarea Philippi (Banias) for a hearing. Wherever Philip and his retinue traveled among his people. A petitioner need only indicate a desire for a decision in a legal dispute and Philip's caravan would immediately stop wherever they were and he would hold court. The summary of Philip's actions is consistent with the "disparate treatment" in Luke 17. Josephus said, "He there ordered the guilty that were convicted to be punished, and absolved those that had been accused unjustly" (*Antiquities* 18.4). Luke said twice, "One shall be seized, the other left" (Luke 17:34-35). Parallels don't come much clearer than that. This typical description of justice, releasing those unjustly accused is the point of judicial tribunals. Determining guilt or innocence, ordering punishment or release, this is the expected result of a trial. Taking Josephus' description at face value, there is no evidence that he was specifically referring to the arrests in Luke 17, but it confirms a normal legal context for the disparate treatment in Luke 17:34-35. The fact that Philip was known for his lightning quick judicial accessibility on any spot of ground in his east-west domain is parallel to Luke 17:24 and Matthew 24:27.

Talmud: How to Conduct an Entrapment

We have Talmudic entrapment procedures used by the rabbis.[126] The Tosefta Sanhedrin disallows entrapment for anyone but an enticer to idolatry. Because of chronology, this record is not strictly evidence but is introduced to illustrate the kinds of law enforcement procedures discussed by the sages, and the kind of nocturnal situation that would facilitate an entrapment

Gays and lesbians were easy pickings, the low-hanging fruit, convenient targets of opportunity for militant law enforcement types like Yohanan b. Zakkai.

with credible witnesses. This relates to the events in Luke 17:34 "in that night." An enticer is a person who persuades people to worship false gods, and the label would have applied to both Jesus and his followers. Berkowitz calls the subsequent punitive action "a properly performed, historically specific rabbinic execution, and that execution is, intriguingly, identified by some scholars as that of Jesus." Tosefta Sanhedrin describes the entrapment of an "enticer," a crime derived from Deuteronomy 13:7-12.

> For all the capital crimes that are in the Torah, they do not entrap except for the enticer. How [do they entrap the enticer]? They send to him two Sages in the inner room, and he sits in the outer room, and they light a candle so that they can see him and hear his voice. And thus they did to Ben Stada in Lod—they appointed against him two Sages and they stoned him.[127]

This rabbinic reference to entrapment in the "inner room" parallels the gospel warning against entrapment in the "inner room" in Matthew 24:26 and Luke 12:3. This intersection of the presumed privacy of the ancient inner room and ancient law enforcement perfectly parallels complaints about government intrusion into the privacy of the bedroom today.

Entrapment undoubtedly goes back as far as kings David and Solomon. It was not a rabbinic invention, but has been a justifiable law enforcement technique throughout history.

Entrapment is quite compatible with the Talmud's picture of Ribaz. His preference for fear over love as a motive for obedience, his interest in capital punishment, and his legal explanation to a magistrate regarding sexual transgression and jurisdictional issues—all these are the picture of law enforcement. The case for a Galilean purity campaign conducted by Ribaz is not an argument from silence. The case for the campaign is circumstantial, but no other known figure had the means, motive and opportunity, not to mention the legal authority and responsibility, to conduct such a campaign.

> ...no other known figure had the means, motive and opportunity, not to mention the legal authority and responsibility, to conduct such a campaign.

We have no Talmudic narrative for this purification campaign of which I am aware. The need for discretion in acknowledging submission to Rome is understandable. The suppression of evidence at Yavneh need not have lasted long, not even to 150 CE. I follow Neusner here.

> [I]t is presumable that in many cases Yoḥanan's opinions have been quietly dropped. We have no reason to suppose a wide selection of Yoḥanan's legal sayings existed at the middle of the second century but then was lost or suppressed.[128]

Neusner insists that nothing was "preserved" about R. Yoḥanan except what his successors, the Hillelites, needed to use. R. Neusner underscores the political coloring of Zakkai's record. To me this suggests that the picture we have of Ribaz was carefully crafted, sanitized of material that was antithetical to the precedent-conscious Hillelites, dangerous to the Jewish people under the newly Christianized Roman imperial power.

The undesirability of Yoḥanan b. Zakkai's example and precedent of vigorous law enforcement and capitulation to Roman authority cannot be overemphasized.

> A story was a precedent and a precedent was binding. No one was willing to "remember" what he could not to begin with believe to be true. So the few ordinances we have are those Gamaliel II and his court transmitted or were unable to suppress.[129]

Catherine Hezser summarized Neusner's transition from biographical studies to single-text redactional studies this way:

> The meager results of this critical biographical approach [to Yoḥanan b. Zakkai] caused Neusner to abandon biographical and historical studies altogether and to concentrate his efforts on the analysis of the redactional character and purpose of single rabbinic documents.[130]

Fortunately, the present thesis doesn't plot a course from a single set of coordinates, but three. The historicity of all three sources has been subjected to considerable scrutiny and found wanting. But when three such disparate sources agree on a matter, this agreement is significant. We triangulate the sources to form a three-dimensional picture of the Pharisees. There are at least six places where the gospels, the Talmud and Josephus agree on the Pharisees. In no particular order, Pharisees

1. exercised law enforcement duties,
2. were involved in politics (governing),
3. sometimes coordinated and planned taking human life,
4. had differing approaches to problem-solving,
5. justified their actions using Scripture, and
6. worked at various levels of government.

Josephus describes the widest range of political activity of the three sources, including protesting, advising and governing at the highest levels. The New Testament contains first-person discussions of Pharisaic judicial and law enforcement activity, a conspiracy to assassinate another Pharisee, pre-arrest warnings about Pharisees and their techniques and mention of various enforcement incident locations. The Talmud describes the region's chief Jewish law enforcement official, his reputation and attitudes, a condensed and multi-layered version of a conflict with a ruler and a specific method used against ideological opponents.

According to the Talmud, Ribaz was concerned with the death penalty, argued that fear was the preferred motivation as opposed to love, and was characterized by bold action. In response to a gentile ruler he justified the execution of an ox, which was not normally subject to Torah. Using the principle of analogy, this could be applied to gentiles in the hands of a resourceful lawyer, to a gentile lesbian, for example.

> [W]hatever we know about Yohanan b. Zakkai has been handed on to us by later generations.... People did not keep alive traditions, sayings, or stories because they were antiquarians, but because they thought them holy or *important*.[131]

We must remember that the sages of Yavneh who took over from R. Yohanan were not ignorant hicks or hapless villagers. They were the best legal minds in the nation. They kept more balls in the air than a constitutional lawyer.

We know from all three sources (Josephus, the gospels and the Talmud) that an entire segment of the Jewish population was zealous for the Law, not just those specifically labeled Zealots. Two prolific Jewish writers were strong advocates for the death penalty for same-sex transgressors. Saul the Pharisee persecuted Jewish heretics with deadly force and was quite hostile to same-sex activity. He wrote that "they which commit such things are worthy of death" (Rom. 1:32). Again, Philo of Alexandria favored the execution of males caught in same-sex activity,

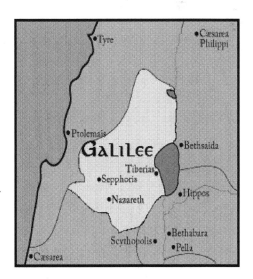

apparently without delay. Transgressing males "should perish unavenged, suffered not to live for a day or even an hour." [132]

Pharisees are recorded as harshly condemning common people, calling them *'am ha-aretz*.[133] By most accounts, Jesus was different from other people. He was apparently a non-conformist, independent in thought and action. He was not the sort of person to whom people in power naturally gravitate unless they think they can use him. And apparently Jesus was not one who could be used, quite the opposite. Other *'am ha-aretz* would likely follow someone similar to Jesus. Any effective campaign against non-conformists would have swept up Jesus followers and a lot of others, including gays and lesbians.

It is important to remember that in the early decades of Christian history, there was no strict line separating Jews and Christians. The early Jesus followers considered themselves Jews, and so did the Jewish authorities. Thus, in his mind Yoḥanan b. Zakkai was not persecuting another religion. He believed he was fighting for the purity of the Jewish people by eliminating Jews unwilling to repent of their sin and their sodomy. For R. Yoḥanan suppressing of gays and lesbians was an in-house, domestic affair.

Waging a campaign to suppress non-conformity could have been relatively manageable in such a small area. At roughly 625 sq. miles, the Galilee was the size of a median U.S. county (622 sq. miles). If R. Yoḥanan had an adequate network of informants, non-conformist targets might have been easy to identify in eighteen years. Following a domestic policy similar to that of the Hasmonean dynasty[134], R. Yoḥanan would not have found it impossible to bring the Galilee further into subjection to Torah, so long as he could persuade the local elders and officials to cooperate. What was true of Pharisee Yoḥanan b. Zakkai late in his career would have characterized him in his early career as well. "Whatever the opposition he faced, Yoḥanan clearly considered himself the possessor of the legitimate internal autonomy available to Israel."[135] R. Yoḥanan threw himself into the task at hand the same way he did at Yavneh, with the same resourceful flexibility.

The Galilee had spent many years separated from Jerusalem's Temple-state leadership. Even a century under Hasmonean rule was not enough. Galilee was a mix of piety and commerce, oppression and prosperity, rural conservatism and messianic turmoil, rebellion and resignation. One thing is sure: for Yoḥanan the Pharisee, the Galilee could never be Jewish enough, could never be orderly enough. With centuries away from the sanctifying influence of Torah, Galilean society was perpetuating all the wrong behaviors, and *every* problem was a problem of Torah, a "social problem." And he had almost two decades to do what the job required.

> From Hillel Yoḥanan would have learned that the sage has the responsibility to concern himself with pressing social problems.... He also would have learned the usefulness of the special decree to deal with a crisis. He decreed changes in law which were far more substantial than the social ordinances of Hillel. He struck out provisions of the Temple cult which men believed were of Mosaic origin.[136]

Such an "everything necessary" attitude did not spring from nothing. The personality portrayed as above Torah at Yavneh had a similar attitude earlier in his career. To many Americans, I suspect Yoḥanan b. Zakkai would seem authoritarian, arrogant and imperious. In the Talmud he is "reasonable" with gentile rulers but harsh with domestic adversaries, e.g., mumbling priests.[137] Some people dismiss his stark portrayal as a kind of rabbinic ideal. I am not a Talmud scholar, but I have a problem with minimizing the portrait of Yoḥanan b. Zakkai's abrasiveness and resort to insult. Pivotal figures in history frequently do not score high in likability. This reputation is typically Shammaite in the Talmud, and the House of Shamma is reputedly the Pharisaic faction that dominated

Israel prior to 70 CE. No known figure was able to wage war against Galilean apostasy better than the leader who lamented, "Galilee, you hate Torah."

It would have been the *'am ha-aretz* who bore the brunt of the campaign to suppress Torah non-observance. Details regarding this campaign were preserved in Q. There are the SBC cities: Sodom, Bethsaida, and Chorazin (Luke 10:12-13/QS 22), whose textual juxtaposition is a clue to what motivated the rejection described. The two Sodom-related cities are condemned for their impenitence.

The Q Source contains a wealth of information pertinent to the themes discussed here. There is the accusation that Jesus is in league with Beelzeboul, who according to the Solomonic pseudepigrapha spreads sodomy. The reference to Solomon and the Queen of the South (Luke 11:19, 31/QS 28) are congruent with the element of cross-border romance in the Couples Material.[138] The Pharisees considered such "race mixing" moral pollution and tried to root out. The mention of Jewish exorcists and Pharisees (Luke 11:19/QS 28 and 34) are evidence of the presence of Pharisees, specifically Hanina b. Dosa and Ribaz. This, of course, is in addition to the story of the Centurion's Servant.

The controversy surrounding two men in one bed has been around for a while. It did not suddenly appear in the aftermath of the Stonewall Uprising or the repeal of DOMA, or the constitutional protection of Marriage Equality. I've tracked a bit of the debate over the two men in verse 34 back over 250 years in English, and as far back as the formation of canonical Luke itself. The debate over verse 35's two women grinding was a little harder to track down, but with the advent of the internet some of the debate is easily accessed by the public.

I would have quit the search for the significance with Zeus and Ganymede except for one thing. While the symbolism for Zeus is present, there is no corresponding symbolism for Ganymede. There is no obvious nearby reference to a cupbearer, no Phrygian cap lying about, no reference to the saga of kidnapping or exaltation.

The lightning and eagles symbolism points to the Galilee Episode more clearly than the symbolic presence of gods and demigods. The ruling of Philip the Tetrarch affected the lives of the gay and lesbian gentiles, rescuing them from execution, just as Zeus intervened in the life of Ganymede, rescuing him from his ordinary fate. In the illustration above, Ganymede's gratitude towards Zeus parallels the gratitude to Philip of gentile gays and lesbians.

Luke-Acts helps us understand the first-century multicultural setting. Remember the black gay official: the Ethiopian eunuch was taught correctly and baptized by Philip the Evangelist (Acts 8). Remember how the Apostle Paul and his companion Barnabas were mistaken for Zeus and Hermes (Acts 14:11-18). And there was Paul's familiarity with the philosophers Epimenides and Aratus (Acts 17:22-28). In addition to a high comfort level with sexual minorities and with contemporary religion and philosophy, there is the active ministry of women in the four daughters of Philip the Evangelist, all of whom "prophesied" (Acts 21:8,9), reminiscent of the oracles of Delphi. The book of Acts is understandably permeated with elements from the Roman religion and pantheon.

Several elements in Luke's Small Apocalypse [139] point to the gay theme. First, the lightning and eagles may refer to either the story of Zeus and Ganymede or, more likely, to the role and ruling of Philip the Tetrarch. Second, between the lighting and eagles is the Jewish gay thematic symbol (17:28, 29).[140] Third are the same-sex couples are near the climax of Luke's Small Apocalypse. The gay male couple is described with a reference to Leviticus, and the lesbian couple being described with an ancient sexual idiom familiar in Hebrew, Latin and Greek. The final element pointing to the sexual theme are the words *in that night*. Any one of these markers, standing alone, would be unpersuasive. But there are four, possibly five, same-sex markers in the space of ten verses.

Remember when I said I was afraid of looking at Q, that it might contain something that would sink my thesis? Well, it did throw me a curve ball. Over a period of a couple of years I noticed that one or another of the four same-sex markers I've written about so much were not in the Q Source. When I noticed it the first time, I ignored it. Maybe I was hoping it would somehow just go away. The second time, I grew more concerned. When a third verse became apparent I realized I would have to figure out why. Why were some of the clearest same-sex markers in Luke 17:28-35 missing from the oldest layers of gospel tradition? The bed, the night, Lot and Sodom— none of these were in the Q Source.

Takeaways: The Galilee Episode

1. In Luke 17:34-35 Jesus talked about two gay and lesbian couples in a "Catch and Release" situation.

2. Instead of the rapture, a historical understanding of these verses is same-sex activity minus divine judgment.

3. The same-sex couples were mixed ethnicity, Jew and gentile.

4. The two couples were on trial for sexual transgression, and were arrested by Pharisees, Jewish law enforcement.

5. Pharisee Yoḥanan b. Zakkai was Prosecutor in the case.

6. Philip the Tetrarch was Presiding Judge, and ruled against the prosecution, ruling that gentiles in his domain were not subject to Jewish Law.

7. The key to unlocking this legal episode is Luke 17:34-35.

8. "The Galilee Episode" refers to the arrests and trial of the same-sex couples referenced in Luke 17.

9. The *Pericope Eiusdem Sexus*, or the Same-Sex Pericope, is Luke 17:28-29 & 34. It was written to underscore the Same-Sex theme already present in the Q Source.

10. The Pharisee Yoḥanan b. Zakkai was active in Upper Galilee at the same time as Jesus and Philip the Tetrarch.

11. Philip successfully raised the status of Bethsaida to imperial polis in 30 CE, which required legal clarification.

12. Prior to 70 CE, Pharisees were non-Levites who policed and helped govern the Jews according to Torah. They were not pastors or theologians, but political functionaries and law enforcement agens.

13. No narrative account of the Same-Sex Couples Trial involving Philip the Tetrarch and Yoḥanan b. Zakkai was written because it was not thematically valuable to Josephus, the Talmudic authorship, or the gospel writers.

14. Even with no narrative, these three sources provide interlocking evidence, which give us a clear picture of the Galilee Episode arrests, trial, and decision.

15. The duplication of the Noah Cycle was to emphasize the anti-homosexual grounds of the arrests of the two couples.

Making the
Same-Sex Pericope

When you compare canonical Luke 17:20-37 with the Q Source, you can see that only the following ten verses are from the older material. What follows is, in English and with the 1551 verse numbering, roughly those ten verses from the Q Sayings Source.

> [20] But on being asked when the kingdom of God is coming, he answered them and said: The kingdom of God is not coming visibly. [21] Nor will one say: Look, here! or: There! For, look, the kingdom of God is within you!

[23] If they say to you: Look, he is in the wilderness, do not go out; look, he is indoors, do not follow. [24] For as the lightning streaks out from Sunrise and flashes as far as Sunset, so will be the Son of Humanity on his day.

[37] Wherever the corpse, there the vultures will gather.

[26] As it took place in the days of Noah, so will it be in the day of the Son of Humanity. [27] For as in those days, they were eating and drinking, marrying and giving in marriage, until the day Noah entered the ark and the flood came and took them all, [30] so will it also be on the day the Son of Humanity is revealed.

[34] There will be two in the field; one is taken and one is left. [35] Two women will be grinding at the mill; one is taken and one is left.

While the *bed*, the *night*, and the Lot Cycle are absent, it's not as though the Galilee Episode itself is missing from the Q Source.

The four elements of the Galilee Episode are present in the older material.

- Pharisee Entrapment (21, 23)
- Pharisee Raids on Same-Sex Couples (34, 35)
- Philip the Tetrarch's Reputation (24)
- Philip's Ruling in the Same-Sex Couples Cases (34, 35)

These four key elements of the Galilee Episode are original to the Q Source. For some time I was at a loss to explain why three details of the same-sex theme, details that were important in my case, were *not* original to Q. The *bed,* where my investigation started, was not originally in Q. *That night* was also not original to Q. The Lot cycle, was also an added element in canonical Luke. Two of the same-sex elements *were* original to Q, *two men* was there, *two women grinding together* was there. *One shall be taken, and the other left,* those two elements were in Q.[141] But a lot of material was added to Q by early scribes to form the gospel of Luke as we have it.

When it came time to figure out why this material wasn't original to Q, I already knew a few things. I knew the Lot cycle had been carefully composed to parallel the Noah cycle. I knew the Couples Couplet had been carefully crafted. From this evidence of construction I had already concluded that their same-sex theme was deliberate.

Then I realized something. These themed verses almost appear in a solid block. The coherence of the block suggested to me that it had been composed and added deliberately.

I believe that the Same-Sex Pericope (*Pericope Eiusdem Sexus*) (Luke 17:28-29, 34), compact and thematically connected, was written by a single scribe. I believe this single authorship is likely, but it is not essential for interpretation. Having an idea of how the passage came into existence is helpful nevertheless. The name I've selected for this scribe has no special significance, although it is a letter of the Hebrew alphabet. I'm calling him Gimel.

The ten verses above are what Gimel, a Lukan[142] scribe, read when the pages came to him. It all looks very familiar, but there is some familiar material missing, missing since it hadn't been written yet. There was at least one other copy of Q circulating. I suspect that the circle of literate scribes was small enough that Gimel may have known the other recipient personally or by reputation. Knowing Gimel's thoughts and concerns is difficult after 2,000 years, what with him being dead and all. Difficult, but not totally impossible.

Comparing Q with canonical Luke, we can make inferences based on what was added and edited. I will describe the two basic steps in the revision process of Luke's small apocalypse, between the Q source and canonical Luke, although the stages and number of edits is likely more. Step One: The Lot cycle was added at the same general time *bed* and *night* appeared in verse 34. Step Two: Some time later other scribes added "distractor" material, including verses 31-33. Very simple, two stages. I don't know how many years this took, or precisely when it happened, but when Q came into the hands of the first Lukan scribes, four key elements of the Galilee Episode were present, and Gimel made the motivation of the raids and entrapment clearer. Later, the document came into the hands of a second group of scribes who made the motivation for that same episode less clear. If the present thesis is correct regarding the precipitating factor, and the Galilee Episode was occasioned by the elevation of Bethsaida to imperial polis, then the year 30 CE is the earliest date possible for the composition of verses 34 and 35. The legal proceedings involving gentile accountability to Torah would depend on how quickly Yoḥanan b. Zakkai launched his test case(s) and how quickly Philip rendered his decision.

We assume that Gimel, the scribe who expanded the older passage, was familiar with the events of Bethsaida and Chorazin. He probably knew that not all of his scribal colleagues would have reason to underscore this judicial furor. Some people would have no interest in preserving the historical memory of these gays and lesbians or the conflict between the Jewish and Roman legal systems.

The Duplication of the Noah Cycle

One of Gimel's biggest tasks seems to have been reproducing the gist of the Noah story, with a modicum of editing. The editing was just enough to clarify the issues that underlay the arrests referenced in Luke 17:34-35. We know this because the words *Sodom* and *Lot* are the most substantive changes. There are three notable differences between the Noah story and the Lot story: the name of the protagonist, the location of the disaster, and the activities prior to the disaster. The most subtle change was in the non-blameworthy human activities prior to the disasters. In a nutshell, the difference between the Noah and Lot cycles pre-disaster activities relate to regulating sexuality. The original Noah cycle included "marrying and giving in marriage," which is absent from the duplication. In the new introduction to the Couples Couplet, Noah became Lot, and the global disaster was localized to Sodom. There is one thing that did not change. There is still no hint of judgment teleology, no clue regarding a *reason* for either the flood or for the fire from heaven. Reasons for divine judgment figured in the Old Testament narrative itself, but not in the Lukan disaster accounts.

Gimel knew why the Lukan couples had been arrested. He knew the legal reason for the seizure of one person and the release of the other. He would have been quite young had he lived during the furor, but in any event it had been big news. There was no way for Gimel to put a finer point on the legal furor without distressing his more traditional fellow scribes. There had been, we assume, sympathy among *'am ha-aretz* for both sides of the conflict.

Now regarding the Couples Couplet: Gimel was nobody's fool. He knew about the raids on the couples, but the text he was reading was a little vague. He knew what could happen in the privacy of the fields, where there are no prying eyes. There was even a law about young virgin women being raped out in a field, a situation where there were no witnesses to hear her cry out (Deut. 22:25-26). A man could bed a young woman in the town, but she might cry out unexpectedly, and that would mean trouble. Discussing the apprehensions in the field was too complicated, and too vague. Then it came to him, a single edit. Cross out *field* and insert *bed*, the *bed* was in Leviticus and the *duo* is masculine. The actual word *men* is not in the text, so the motive for the apprehensions would be clearer, but not glaring. He looked over what he had written. "They will be able to see it now," he whispered.

In changing *field* to *bed*, Gimel had disturbed a parallelism in the Q text. Knowing whether he was aware of this parallelism and its significance is not essential. But in the original version, an outside/inside parallelism was present in Q 17:23 and 34.

> If they say to you: Look, he is in the wilderness, do not go out; look, he is indoors, do not follow.

> There will be two in the field; one is taken and one is left. Two women will be grinding at the mill; one is taken and one is left.

In Q, *wilderness* parallels *field*, and *indoors* parallels *grinding*. The edit suggests that at this point Gimel was most interested in the clarity of his sexual focus.

And the two women grinding together at the mill? We don't know for sure which version was Q's, with or without the mill. Matthew has the mill, Luke does not. I believe *mill* was Matthew's addition. Matthew seems to have a pattern of added words. But even if the mill were originally in Q, that was easy enough to remedy. Just delete the *muloni* and you have two women grinding together, and not a mill in sight—not a mill most people would likely use for wheat or oats. We know from Plutarch's "*grind, mill grind*" that the presence or absence of the word *mill* is not conclusive. We know from Horace's "*rather than grind some husband's private mill*" that even when used together they can point to sex.

We have *muloni* (mill) in Matthew but no *muloni* in Luke. When we see differences between the Synoptic Gospels we must ask, "What was the concern that prompted that edit?" If someone believes that clarity and eliminating ambiguity was the motivation, the follow-up questions are, "If the original version was ambiguous, then what were the possible meanings of the ambiguous version? And for what reason were other meanings eliminated?"

Q's Noah account read "*marrying and giving in marriage.*" The couples Gimel was talking about weren't allowed to marry in this part of the empire. References to marriage were problematic. He apparently thought it better to avoid anything overtly related to courting, romance or marriage. He wrote for some time. Eventually he stopped writing and read aloud the connector material he had created.

> Likewise, also as it was in the days of Lot; they did eat, they drank, they bought, they sold, they planted, they builded; But the same day that Lot went out of Sodom it rained fire and brimstone from heaven, and destroyed them all. I tell you, there shall be two in one bed; the one shall be taken, and the other shall be left. There shall be two women grinding together; one shall be taken, and the other left.

Gimel was pleased. The targets had lived normal lives, eating and drinking just as everyone else. They had normal commercial livelihoods buying and selling. They planned for the future, planting and building for themselves and for generations to come.

Unlike the days of Noah he days of Lot do not include marriage, but the story ends in disaster nevertheless.

Rereading the text, he thought about those who had been executed, and about the lucky ones Philip absolved. Now they would be remembered by posterity. He lay there and wondered if people would understand the separation, why some were seized and others were released. He had been a child during the worst of the campaign, and the victims were gone. He remembered the stories, wondering if there was some detail to add. He was no longer satisfied with what he had written.

Gimel was almost asleep when his eyes opened. "More tolerable in that day for Sodom." He remembered. Perfect. How could he forget? He knew he had to write it down before he slept. *Why didn't I remember this?* In the margin he wrote the word "νυκτὸς." *Night.*

Gimel had done his best. Before he died, the manuscript had already become someone else's responsibility. Once it was out of his hands, he couldn't control what others did with it. He knew he respected what was written, adding only congruent material, making only small changes, nothing that would change the essential direction of the text.

The *PES* is only three verses. There is other material in the Small Apocalypse that is also not in Q. All the verses that point away from the gay theme, or dilute it, they are also Lukan additions, but they are subsequent to the *Pericope Eiusdem Sexus*.

Gays & Lesbians in Luke and the Q Apocalypse

In the Gay Apocalypse there are some verses that have nothing to do with the gay theme outlined here. In my early research I was still in preaching mode, conceiving my task as verse-by-verse exposition, such as J. Vernon McGee or Chuck Smith. I conceived of the text as a coherent whole, and I wanted to understand the alternative interpretations they offered. When my thesis first began to take shape, I knew I would have to explain how these other verses related to the emerging gay theme. Initially I was afraid I'd have to torture the verses to make them support the gay theme, and I detested the habit of some Bible believers of torturing scripture for a coerced confession. When there's a difference of opinion in the Bible, that sounds like real life to me. The world is filled with conflicting opinions.

While I was dreading the possibility of torturing the text, I wondered if the Q Source might shed some light on my problem. Looking at Q was the beginning of my exploration of the historical situation, a journey away from a narrow approach to Biblical research that eventually

> ### Pericope Eiusdem Sexus
> ### Luke 17:28-29, 34
>
> Likewise also as it was in the days of Lot; they did eat, they drank, they bought, they sold, they planted, they builded;
>
> But the same day that Lot went out of Sodom it rained fire and brimstone from heaven, and destroyed them all.
>
> I tell you, in that night
> there shall be two men in one bed;
> the one shall be taken,
> and the other shall be left.
>
> © 2018, Ronald Goetz

included the Talmud and Josephus. Q used to hold little interest for me except for a New Testament survey course where the professor briefly discussed the two-source hypothesis. Even though I was studying with a purpose, I feared that Q would uncover some unseen obstacle, something that would pierce the hull and sink my thesis. I felt intimidated by an area of study almost unknown to me.

But an inquiry into Q, searching for potential insights was the next logical step toward an adequate exegesis. I didn't know what Q might do.[143]

One of the first things I discovered was something I had not anticipated: The Healing of the Centurion's Servant was in the Q source. Jennings and Liew describe the now well-known same-sex relationship in the story (Matt. 8:5-13).[144] Later I discovered the connection of the Beelzeboul Accusation with sodomy in the pseudepigrapha.[145] These two elements in Q were part of the same-sex theme I'd found in Luke 17. Discovering there were three distinct elements of same-sex material in Q told me I was on the right path. This was totally unexpected.

The same-sex connection of the Beelzeboul Accusation (Luke 11:15) is not widely known. Solomon lore figures highly in this section of gospel tradition. One ancient text, which was a favorite among exorcists, was the pseudepigraphal *Testament of Solomon* (*ToS*). In the *Testament of Solomon,* the king interviews many of the demons of hell, including the chief demon Beelzeboul. At one point Beelzeboul answers Solomon about his activities, "I inspire men with envy, and murder, and for wars and sodomy" (*ToS* 27). Typical of ancient documents, textual questions make this passage uncertain. But given the Jewish exorcists in Jesus' original audience and the evident popularity of extra-biblical Solomon lore in Luke 11:31, it is possible that Jesus critics believed he was a subject of the chief demon who spread sodomy among men.

The Later, Non-Q Material

The 18 verses of the Small Apocalypse of canonical Luke are mainly Q material, ten verses. In the official 2001 version of the *Sayings Source Q*, the Small Apocalypse consists of ten verses.[146] Only eight verses were added to Q by later hands. Those eight verses, while a part of canonical Luke, are *not* found in Sayings

Gospel Q. We have already discussed three of those eight verses, but I will now show all eight.

> [22]And he said unto the disciples, The days will come, when ye shall desire to see one of the days of the Son of man, and ye shall not see it.

> [25]But first must he suffer many things, and be rejected of this generation.

> [28] *Likewise also as it was in the days of Lot; they did eat, they drank, they bought, they sold, they planted, they builded;*

> [29] *But the same day that Lot went out of Sodom it rained fire and brimstone from heaven, and destroyed them all.*

> [31] In that day, he which shall be upon the housetop, and his stuff in the house, let him not come down to take it away: and he that is in the field, let him likewise not return back.

> [32] Remember Lot's wife!

> [33] Whosoever shall seek to save his life shall lose it; and whosoever shall lose his life shall preserve it.

> [34] *I tell you, in that night* there will be two men in *one bed.*

This non-Q material is not singled out arbitrarily. Labeling it "non-Q" simply recognizes that is not in Matthew; that it is what the Lukan authorship[147] added to the original materials. (I have italicized the material in the *Pericope Eiusdem Sexus*.)

Of all the Lukan additions to QS60, one of the shortest is Luke 17:34a. The edit is a total of five Greek words: λέγω ὑμῖν ταύτῃ τῇ νυκτὶ, "I tell you" and "in that night." The word *bed* in "two men will be in one bed" is also an edit, a careful Lukan creation, and that "two men in a *field*" is how Q read originally.[148] The Noah cycle was original to Q, but not the Lot and Sodom material. Like "two men in one bed," the Lot cycle is a carefully crafted parallel. There are already two pairs of same-sex adults in the narrative, one pair in the field and one pair grinding together. Gimel the redactor, after crafting the Sodom scene, and after changing the location of a grammatically masculine pair from a field to a bed, finally specifies *night* as the time this all occurred. The sexual content of the *Pericope Eiusdem Sexus* (*PES*) was deliberate. Each element of the *PES* (the Lot and Sodom material, the *night*, and the *bed*) points toward the distinctive sexual theme.

The *Pericope Eiusdem Sexus* and the SBC Cities

(I have gone into technical detail already, but what follows is pretty dense. You may want to skip ahead to the next subhead.) Bethsaida and Chorazin and the Couples Couplet are both introduced with the word λέγω (*lego*). This may be a scribal redaction habit. This pattern uses the word λέγω, which means "I declare to you." *Lego* is an authoritative word. Imagine someone underscoring the importance of what they're saying, "I promise you," "You can take it from me," or "I'm not kidding." Q's pre-existing same-sex material (*two in a field* and *two women grinding*) was brought into sharper focus by the Lot & Sodom material and the addition of *night* and *bed*. The word *lego* is used in the following two places. First, the nighttime bedding is introduced with the word *lego*. That word is also present in Q 10:12, which introduces the Galilean cities of Bethsaida and Chorazin. Based on a careful study of the wording, John Kloppenborg concluded that "10:12 is one of the best candidates for a saying *created* by the editor of Q."[149] Note that we are talking about two different redactions, the first is a redaction *within* the Q document, the second is a later redaction made *to* what became canonical Luke.

The redaction of Q 10:12 introduces Sodom into the discussion, seemingly from nowhere. Second, it contains the previously mentioned *lego*. Verse 12 was created and placed by a

Q redactor to link two preexisting sections. This redaction placed *Sodom* into Q itself. The first section instructs the listeners to travel light and to receive people's hospitality. The second section contains woes on two specific cities, Bethsaida and Chorazin.

> But I say unto you (λέγω), that it shall be more tolerable in that day for Sodom, than for that city. Woe unto thee, Chorazin! woe unto thee, Bethsaida!

The reason Kloppenborg's observation is important is the association of the Bethsaida and Chorazin with Sodom. A scribe was telling readers something important about Bethsaida and Chorazin. This connection can be easy to miss. Both of these redactions are connected with the mention of Sodom, which raises the possibility of some connection between the scribe redacting Q and the scribe creating the *PES*.

Subhead Placement

In an English language Bible today, Sodom is often visually separated from the cities of Bethsaida and Chorazin by a subhead with some variation on "Woe to Unrepentant Cities." If I am reading him correctly, Kloppenborg implies that Sodom in verse 12 was originally connected with Bethsaida and Chorazin in verse 13, and not the cities which rejected the Jesus emissaries in verses 10-11. To see the difference this editorializing makes, here is Luke 10:10-13 (NRSV) with the non-canonical subhead as it is, then placed differently.

> [10] But whenever you enter a town and they do not welcome you, go out into its streets and say, [11] 'Even the dust of your town that clings to our feet, we wipe off in protest against you. Yet know this: the kingdom of God has come near.' [12] I tell you, on that day it will be more tolerable for Sodom than for that town.
>
> **Woes to Unrepentant Cities**   (Usual version)

In the example above, the placement of the subhead guides the reader to associate the mention of Sodom with the idea of rejecting the message. In the following text box, the placement of the subhead would guide the reader to associate Sodom with the cities of Bethsaida and Chorazin.

Woes to Unrepentant Cities

[12] I tell you, on that day it will be more tolerable for Sodom than for that town.[13] "Woe to you, Chorazin! Woe to you, Bethsaida! For if the deeds of power done in you had been done in Tyre and Sidon, they would have repented long ago, sitting in sackcloth and ashes.

(Suggested revision)

The NRSV's original placement of the editorial heading "Woes to Unrepentant Cities" was a problematic editorial decision. It is one thing to associate Sodom with an attitude of rejection. It is quite another to associate a specific Old Testament city with two specific Galilean cities, when one of them is undergoing official renewal and expansion. The NIV itself removes the quotation marks from verse 12, indicating that Jesus did not mention Sodom in this passage. This is consistent with the idea that Christian scribes emended the text after the reported events.

To summarize: both Luke 10:12-13 and Luke 17:28-29, 34-35 refer to the Galilee Episode. Both passages refer to Sodom, and they are the only mentions of Sodom in Luke. Both passages are neutral or slightly positive toward the symbolic city. Both passages contain the authoritative declaration, "I tell you." The mention of Sodom seems to be a flag marking a significant same-sex element of the Galilee Episode.

"I tell you, on that day" Luke 10:12a

"I tell you, in that night" Luke 17:34a

The mention of Sodom in 10:12, a redaction within the Q source, only *seems* to come out of nowhere. It is related to the conflict at Bethsaida and Chorazin itself. While rounding up a posse or during a trial, the Pharisees compared their targets to the menacing crowd in Sodom. When the Pharisees used the Sodom dog whistle, the city became relevant to the inhospitable rhetoric of rejection pummeling the Q community.

When invoked *together*, Sodom and Gomorrah symbolize rebellion and judgment. However, when Sodom *alone* is mentioned it conjures up the details of Lot's story, the angelic visitors and the threat of man-on-man rape. Centuries later the events in Sodom gave rise to the English words *sodomy* and *sodomite*. Sodom by itself is mentioned Luke 10:12 and 17:29, not Sodom and Gomorrah together. For this, and for other reasons as well, the assumption that judgment is the theme of Luke's Small Apocalypse is incorrect. The story's same-sex drama is used as a signal in both chapters. The first instance, in Luke 10, is within Q itself. The second instance of Sodom (in Luke 17) was added between Q and canonical Luke. In neither occurrence is there a hint of reproach or culpability attached. This lack of reproach has baffled many readers.

Significance of the Two Sodom Additions

Thus, the mentions of Sodom in Luke were added by two different scribes, and not only do they appear without overtones of culpability or judgment, but the mention in Luke 10:12 is mildly positive. "But I say unto you, that it shall be more tolerable in that day for Sodom." As it happens, the first Sodom reference was added near the Bethsaida and Chorazin rejection episode, and the second addition was to the nighttime separation of the same-sex couples. Let me underscore this: *Sodom was added twice to Luke, once before the mention of Bethsaida and Chorazin, and later before the mention of the gay and lesbian couples.*

Symbolic meanings have built up around some Biblical locations such as Babylon and Egypt, even Jerusalem, because of historical associations. But 2,000 years ago, only one of the SBC cities had a "reputation." At the time, the lesser-known cities had no religious reputation of which we are aware. Sodom, however, had a bad reputation. Their mention is only in Q, and they are now associated with two things: Rejecting the Jesus messengers, and Sodom.

We must think about why the SBC cities appear together, three cities in two verses, within 17 words of each other. I believe that the Pharisees orchestrated the events of Bethsaida and Chorazin using the Sodom dog whistle, pointing at the *'am ha-aretz* Jesus followers as though they were red meat. This makes two passages, and possibly three, where Jesus, his followers and Sodom appear together: first in Bethsaida and Chorazin, second in Luke's Gay Apocalypse, and finally in the Beelzeboul Accusation. It's as though someone in the Lukan authorship was saying, "We may be Sodomites, but Sodom will be better off in the end than you!" In Luke 10:12 and 17:29 Sodom is a flag, a thematic cue added for our benefit.

A similar in-your-face turnabout is flaunted in Luke 11:31, where the dark-skinned Queen of the South is paired with immoral King Solomon to later rise up to denounce "this generation." A sexually immoral, forbidden pairing is used to shame the Pharisees. Using both Sodom and the Queen of the South, Q rebukes the Pharisees using what is despised and notorious.

The Necessity of the Sodom Flag

Regarding Luke 10:13, questions might arise as to why the events at Bethsaida and Chorazin required the Sodom flag in verse 12. It became necessary to add the Sodom flags for two reasons: the passage of time and a change in geographic location. If I refer to My Lai and Abu Graib, geography, time and ideology will affect reader comprehension. If I refer to Aldersgate and Azusa Street, the group of people who will get the reference are also limited. And when the references are even more remote, as in Kafr Qasim and Deir Yassin, or Ludlow and Matewan, the subsets of the demographic subsets who will understand becomes smaller and smaller. Unless you're a certain age, religion, nationality or political persuasion, there are some references you won't get automatically.

At one time (the decade or so following 30 CE) there were probably thousands of people who understood the pairing of Bethsaida and Chorazin and their connection with Philip and R. Yoḥanan and with gays and lesbians. But as years passed, and as the original record (the Q source) migrated hundreds of miles, fewer people remembered or knew of the events at Bethsaida and Chorazin. Realizing this, an anonymous scribe eventually added the Sodom reference.

This specific reference to Sodom eventually took two different paths, one which resulted in Luke 10:12 and the other in Matthew 10:15. In Luke it remained on a path to specificity, to concrete events. In Matthew, however, the scribes directed it away from historicity and toward ideology and futurism (Matt 10:15). Luke kept to the *events* of Sodom, Matthew introduced a *pattern* of judgment by adding the sister city Gomorrah. The authors of Luke-Acts were more interested in history than the authors of Matthew, who were inclined toward futurism.

This difference in how Lukan and Matthean scribes used the Q source is not the only difference here. There were also differences within the Lukan train of scribes itself. Scribes subsequent to Gimel did not appreciate how he highlighted the conflict between R. Yoḥanan and Philip which resulted in splitting up same-sex couples. They did not delete what he had written, but what they added minimized its impact. Considering the passage of time and the subtlety of Gimel's work, whether this was deliberate or not is unclear. Preferring deliberation to ignorance, I am assuming they knew what they were doing.

An Eight-Verse Rebuttal

Just as the story of the Woman taken in Adultery (*Pericope Adulterae*) in John had great utility, so too the eight verses that pepper Luke 17:20-37 have utility in several issues concerning the early church: the delayed Parousia (v 22), the Christ's omniscient prediction of crucifixion (v 25), and other moral, ethical and spiritual applications (vv 31, 32, and 33). None of them pertains to the gay theme, although the stylistically jarring imperative to "Remember Lot's wife!" (v 32) touches on the Genesis story. The absence of the eight verses from the earliest strata of tradition means they are, by definition, Lukan redactions.

Redaction itself is not an issue. Gimel's *PES* is a redaction, and the later distractor material is expansion and redaction also. What we're trying to do here is understand the different reasons behind the redactions, and the order in which they were composed.

There is a reason Gimel decided to attach pointedly gay-themed material right here. It was the original reading of Q's verses 34 and 35: "Two men will be in a field; one is seized, the other is left. Two women will be grinding together; one is seized, the other left." The reason for the Pharisee raids and Philip's intervention were already present in the same-sex Couples Couplet (arrests while in the field and while grinding together, and in the disparate treatment of the targets). But, as preserved in Q, these details were subtle. Gimel added his focusing material to preexisting Galilee Episode material.

Even the refinement and focus provided by the *Pericope Eiusdem Sexus* was almost too subtle. The anonymous scribe we're calling Gimel had crafted two elements to match the Q material in style and content. First, the Lot and Sodom material, second, "two men will be in *a field"* was edited. The third, adding *in that night*, unmistakably focused the revised passage's sexual content. Without the words *in that night* preachers could have objected, "Who knows? Maybe they were just napping. I often nap during the day."

The phrase *in that night* is significant in another way. It appears nowhere else in the New Testament. The technical term for the singular use of a word in a text is *hapax legomenon*. In Luke 17:20-37 alone, the word *day* or *days* appears nine times. Imagine, you're reading along, "… days… days… day… days… day… days… day… day… day… night." [150] It has a certain stopping power. If you were reading the passage for the first time, you might pause momentarily when you came to the word *night*. In the age of Galileo, rapture proponents are forced to interpret the phrase *in that night* less literally. It's no wonder that Scofield Bible preachers had to assure their flocks there was no hanky-panky going on in the passage, with two men in one bed at night and all.

When discussing Luke 17, traditionalists label the overall theme divine judgment. This, despite the fact that the text nowhere refers to judgment, God's intervention or any sin. The overriding theme of Luke's Small Apocalypse is not judgment, but judgmental*ism*. The historical event preserved there is similar to a grain

> A more appropriate understanding of the Couples Material is same-sex activity *minus* divine judgment.

of sand in an oyster, an episode of primate judgmentalism. A more appropriate understanding of the Couples Material is same-sex activity *minus* divine judgment.

Technically, Luke 17:20-37 is not an apocalypse since it does not deal with the judgment of God. I have considered searching for a better label, but for ease of reference I have retained the "apocalypse" label. If you were the Jewish homosexual seized late at night in order to be tried and executed by authorities, it might feel like the end of the world, and for you it probably was. The raid would be a shock, but that's how raids are. Successful law enforcement raids are by definition sudden, and often take place at night.

Regarding those distractor verses in Luke's small apocalypse: in contemporary jury trials, when a hostile witness has emotionally effective testimony, I've heard that defense attorneys have a technique for making that testimony less effective. The simple phrase "objection, your honor" interrupts the momentum of a witness's story. Even groundless objections which the judge will certainly overrule still disrupt emotionally effective testimony.

When the text left Gimel's hands it was powerful testimony regarding the motive for Pharisee vice raids in Bethsaida and Chorazin. Whether the distractor material added after Gimel's *Pericope Eiusdem Sexus* was a deliberate obfuscation or were simply attempts to find a good home for snippets of Jesus lore, we can't know for sure. But in either case the material did distract. The accreted material often attracted more attention than the historical core of the *PES*. Decades after the events, the exhortation "Remember Lot's wife" was more useful in preaching than confusing stuff like "one was taken and the other left." From the perspective of subsequent scribes, only the inevitable dissenters would profit from reminders about officials who might entrap them or plan raids. Encouraging people toward introspection, self-examination and repentance, as personally valuable as these practices are, is also a convenient technique to draw people's attention away from awkward social inequities.

Ancient intellectuals debated, much as today, the acceptability of same-sex relationships. Greek intellectuals lined up, for and against. Roman writers weighed in, pro and con. New Testament scribes were subject to the same diversity of opinion as others. The author of the *Pericope Eiusdem Sexus* hinted in the strongest terms possible the acceptability of gays and lesbians, that there were gays and lesbians among Jesus' persecuted followers. Sodom was the "X marks the spot" drawn on the map of Luke 10 and 17.

The author of the *PES* only hinted? Yes, Gimel only hinted. Good people have always differed on issues of morality, from perceived strictness to perceived laxity. The same players who debated the *Pericope Adulterae* would have debated the *Pericope Eiusdem Sexus*, had it survived intact or been written more plainly. There was probably such a debate before canonical Luke entered circulation. Scribes different from Gimel were confronted with the implications of his *PES* in a text, and they felt at liberty to add to it but not subtract. Unable to allow the implications of the testimony to stand unchallenged, they sprinkled the text with verses 20-22, 25, and 31-33. They repeated "objection, your honor" until the meaning of Gimel's text was nearly drowned out.

Allow me to recap. I am condensing a composition process of possibly decades into three steps. We start with the Q document, which took an unknown period to form. Then, we have the *Pericope Eiusdem Sexus* which develops the preexisting images of two men in a field and two women grinding together less ambiguously, more clearly sexual. Finally, we have a series of scribal "objections" which have drawn our attention away from historical events toward such significant issues as self-seeking, the delayed parousia and the Crucifixion.

Making the Pericope Eiusdem Sexus

I propose that an unrecognized unit exists, Luke 17:28-29, 34. This unit was added to QS60 to 1) form a bridge between the Noah materials and the Couples Couplet, and 2) crystallize the *eiusdem sexus*[151] elements already present in Q. I call this unit the *Pericope Eiusdem Sexus*, or The Same-Sex Pericope.

Gimel the scribe, being a redactor, historian and probably a group leader, recognized in *two in a field* and *two women grinding together* surviving evidence of sexual orientation, and knew the reason for the differing post-arrest treatment. To highlight these preexisting facts, a three-part bridge was constructed, consisting of the Sodom material, the "one bed" edit and the time of day indicator. Some things are more often done at night than during the day. For privacy some primates have more sex at night, and raids on unprepared targets are more effective at night.

The facts of the Galilean Episode were not generated by the additional material. Prior to adding the *Pericope Eiusdem Sexus*, four elements of the historical Galilee Episode were already recorded. First, the warnings against entrapment and raids; second, the lightning and eagles symbolism; third, the presence of two gendered couples and fourth, the disparate treatment of those arrested. The *PES* likewise did not add the reason for the raids, sexual activity between gay and lesbian couples. The *PES* simply accentuated facts already in evidence. Even without the Lot and Sodom material, the time of day cue, and two men located specifically in one bed, clues to the purification campaign were already present.

Why does Luke include the Lot and Sodom material, but Matthew does not? Why does Luke have the pair in a *bed*, and not in a *field*, the way Matthew does? Why does Luke specify that the action occurs at night? Don't throw up your hands and exclaim, "Who knows?" The answer is relatively simple. One scribe supplied more information to the passage because of his historical knowledge, and subsequent scribes tried to "clarify" the passage with additions of their own because of their theological objections. The debate is between history and theology, between a record and a prediction, between people living life and people making rules.

A few last words about those men in Luke 17:34. Q scholars believe that the original couplet began with the somewhat controversial verse 36. "Two men shall be in the field; the one shall be taken, and the other left." If the Q experts are right, then Gimel also moved the δυο out of the αγρω and into the κλίνης μιᾶς, the *two* people from a *field* to *one bed*. And this is how the two earliest codices put it: in Luke 17:34 codices Vaticanus and Sinaiticus read one *bed*, and do not mention the *field*.

> A first-century version of "Catch and Release" is the story behind Luke 17:34-35.
>
> [R. Yoḥanan] had directed apprehensions which included two gentile homosexuals, one male and one female, and been forced to "catch and release" the gentile detainees.

The reappearance of *two men in a field* (v 36) later in the history of manuscripts was a continuation of Yohanan b. Zakkai's original moral controversy. Readers were alerted by scribes to the possible return of Q's two men to the original vicinity. These scribes did not have learned journals in which to publish their concerns. I suspect scribbling Matthew 24:40 in the margin of the text was a scribal way of nudging later scribes to make changes when circumstances allowed. I don't know if the final solution of these later scribes included the eventual elimination of two men or simply keeping two men on the margins.

Interpretive Coherence of the Gay Theme

When we acknowledge the presence of the gay theme, a simple solution emerges for several ongoing controversies concerning the passage.

"Should I stay or should I go?" There is continuing debate over several major implications of the passage, including whether it is better to be left or to be taken. This has been interpreted many ways. In this context John S. Kloppenborg quotes C.H. Dodd's *Parables of the Kingdom* (p. 64), "It is not even clear whether the one taken or the one left has the better lot."

"Vultures, vultures everywhere" or *"Houston, the eagle has landed."* Steven L. Bridge, professor at St. Joseph's College in Maine, points to the generally clear distinction between αετοι (eagles) and γυπες (vultures) in classical Greek, and he supports the *eagles* rendering. Eagles often symbolize deliverance in both the Old Testament and classic Greek literature, whereas vultures are almost always, first and foremost, scavengers of carcasses. Bridge connects the lightning and the eagles to the religious story of Zeus and Ganymede. This connection possibly suggests a Roman gay theme indicator in Luke 17, the other being Jewish. Jews and gentiles were Luke's dual audiences.

"Well, if that isn't déjà vu all over again." A third question for some involves the inexplicability of the double tradition of the Noah and Sodom cycles. If the theme of the passage is simply the suddenness of judgment, then the lavish attention spent on creating the Sodom cycle is mysterious.

The passage's intent is not prediction and the theme is not divine judgment. The origin of this particular Q material warned people of predawn raids targeting same-sex couples, and the use of legal entrapment techniques which included lying and deception to lure the unsuspecting to prearranged locations. The Pharisees targeted the couples because of their sexual orientation in the first place, but that was not the basis for their disparate treatment. There was a very practical reason why some gay and lesbian individuals being seized, and others being released: overlapping legal jurisdictions.

There are two major reasons why generations of Christian interpreters missed the explanation for the disparate treatment of the couples. One we have already discussed: the assumption that the passage was about divine judgment. God's grounds for treating people differently was an automatic concern. The second reason concerns the habit of harmonizing Bible passages.

There is another New Testament passage with which traditional interpreters concern themselves when approaching Luke 17. The gospel of Matthew develops the "false messiah" idea in chapter 24. There are no false messiahs in Luke 17. The actual phrase "false Christs" (ψευδόχριστοι, *pseudochristoi*) is found in canonical Matthew 24:24 but nowhere in Luke. *False christs* were imported into Luke from Matthew after the canonization process was finished. Harmonization and Inerrancy strike again.

I don't know if anyone ever considered that the reason for the Great Separation in Luke 17 might be based on the Jew-gentile distinction. If a theologian assumes the passage is about judgment, and God is the one judging, this reason wouldn't even come up. Paul wrote, "There is neither Jew nor Greek" (Gal. 3:28). "For he is our peace, who hath made [Jews and gentiles] one, and hath broken down the middle wall of partition between us" (Eph. 2:14). If God is the agent of judgment in the stories of Noah and Lot, and God makes no distinction between Jews and Greeks, then the grounds for distinction in the Great Separation wouldn't be one between Jews and gentiles. But in Luke 17 God is *not* an agent of judgment. Law enforcement is the agent of judgment, but not

God's judgment. One was seized and the other left because one was Jewish and the other was gentile. "In real life" only one of them was subject to Jewish law.

Lightning and Mangled Eagles?

I will return for a moment to the possible Zeus and Ganymede symbolism. The origins and meaning of the lightning and the eagles have long been a matter of difficulty for interpreters. Should the word αετοι be rendered *eagles* or *vultures* in Luke 17:37? Kloppenborg, the grandfather of Q scholarship, believes it is impossible to know the ultimate origin of the eagle proverb, and says that "Its ominous tone is in keeping with the threatening and dark metaphors which surround it." But having said that, he is noncommittal. After recounting several interpretations, including those of Bultmann and Jeremias, Kloppenborg writes,

> Whether Q 17:37 is an authentic saying, threatening or otherwise, is impossible to say; Jesus may well have adapted or repeated wisdom sayings such as Job 39:30. Its "original" function is impossible to recover because we have no way of establishing its original interpretive context.... All that can reasonably be discussed is the proverb as it occurs in its present literary context.[152]

The "present literary context" may be changing. If the present thesis is correct, and Luke 17:34-35 refers to mixed-ethnicity same-sex couples targeted by Pharisee morality police who were forced to "catch and release" the non-Jewish transgressors, then we have indeed discovered the passage's "original interpretive context." In conjunction with the SBC cities, the *lightning* and the *eagles* come into the immediate proximity of Philip the Tetrarch, whose jurisdiction included Bethsaida. Just as Zeus dispatched the eagle which snatched up Ganymede and delivered him from his ordinary mortal fate, so too Philip snatched up the gay and lesbian gentiles, delivering them from their fated execution.

If Kloppenborg's "original function" of the eagle imagery is in fact recoverable and symbolized in Philip's interventional ruling on behalf of his non-Jewish subjects, then we must explain why the verbiage surrounding the lightning seems irrelevant. I suggest a possibility. Q scholars believe that the lightning and eagle imagery were originally together as preserved in Matthew. This imagery may once have been more condensed, more clearly referred to Philip the Tetrarch. The same impulse that caused the Small Apocalypse to be peppered with distractor verses could have prompted the Lukan separation of the lightning and the eagles. But this is not essential to the argument. The identification of the same-sex couples, the Pharisaic role in the entrapments and raids, and the intervention of Philip are not affected by the meaning of the lightning and eagles imagery.

The word *parousia* is quite significant in the context of Philip the Tetrarch and Luke 17:34-35. In classical Greek, *parousia* usually refers to an official's physical presence, to the anticipated arrival of a royal personage, a formal occasion. Non-Jewish homosexuals held in custody by Pharisee officials in Bethsaida and Chorazin awaiting the official visit of Philip the Tetrarch were anticipating such an arrival literally, his *parousia*. "In Hellenistic Greek it was used for the arrival of a ruler at a place."[153]

The Matthew 24:27 passage uses the word *parousia*. "For just as the lightning comes from the east and flashes even to the west, so will the coming of the Son of Man be." In contrast, Luke 17:24 does *not* contain the word *parousia*. "For as the lightning, that lighteneth out of the one part under heaven, shineth unto the other part under heaven; so shall also the Son of man be in his day." This would be consistent with the postulated attempts by certain post-Gimel Lukan scribes to obscure the historical events of the Galilee episode. In this scenario, these scribes 1) separated the symbolism of lightning and eagles, 2) peppered the *Pericope Eiusdem Sexus* with valuable but off-topic new material and 3) eliminated the Philip-related *parousia* terminology. The words "part under heaven" are used twice in Luke, and refers to a piece of ground, which has definite territorial connotations.

We have two words with official associations. We have *parousia* (*appearing, coming* or *visitation*) in Matthew but not in Luke. And we have the less familiar word *paralēmphthēsetai* (*taken* or *seized*), twice in Luke 17 and repeated again in Matthew 24. There is a cluster of official words and Roman iconography here. Originally the cluster reflected details derived from the legal, jurisdictional wrangling between Yoḥanan and Philip.

Decades passed. A few hand-copied records (the Q Source) moved long distances, beginning in Galilee and ending up in places probably as close as the Decapolis and Syrian Antioch and as far away as Asia Minor or Rome. With all this traveling, the significance of some references became obscure to some of the text's new readers. Despite the obscurity, not all readers were ignorant of the events described. The preservation of two same-sex couples, several legal words (*seized, parousia, part under heaven*) and two symbols from Roman iconography (*lightning* and *eagles*) in the earliest tradition underscored the relevance of Philip and the cities of Bethsaida and Chorazin in the oldest traditions.

From the inciting events until now, Luke 17:34-35 has been the site of turmoil related to gays and lesbians. First, Yoḥanan b. Zakkai waged a purity campaign targeting homosexuals, and forward-looking rabbis obscured his details. A few Christian scribes preserved this campaign memory, but few were inclined to publicize homosexuals among Jesus followers. Some of them obscured the clarity introduced by Gimel. The later appearance of "two men in a field" in the margins of Luke manuscripts shows that some Christian scribes would not let the issue die. This back-

and-forth continued, and what began as two foundationally strategic cover-ups became a case of total denial.

The comments of Jesus in Luke 17:34-35 reflect enormous solidarity with gays and lesbians. He compared the inhabitants of Sodom favorably, compared to the people who cooperated with the death penalty campaign against gays and lesbians. Jesus implicitly celebrated Philip the Tetrarch, the champion of independent tribal diversity. Every tribe was independent of other tribes, free to govern itself according to its own laws and customs--so long as everyone paid their taxes and Rome got its share.

Jesus commemorates the independence of gentile gays and lesbians from Torah restrictions on their sexuality. From this discussion it would be incorrect to describe Philip as a champion of gay rights. He did not contravene the Pharisee's application of Torah against Jewish gays and lesbians. He left it to the Jews themselves to sort that out. What he did was prevent Jewish leaders from imposing Torah on gentile gays and lesbians.

Takeaways: The Same-Sex Pericope

1. All the changes introduced by Luke 17:28-29, 34 are sexual.

2. The Lot Cycle carefully duplicates the Noah Cycle with three differences.

3. Those three changes solve the puzzle of motivation in the careful duplication of verses 26-27 in verses 28-29.

4. The Bible character was changed from Noah to Lot; the location was changed from the entire world to Sodom; the references to marriage in the Noah cycle were eliminated.

5. The phrase *in that night* was added.

6. The neutral word *field* was changed to *bed*, a more suggestive location for *two men* at *night*.

7. Distractor material, which included verses 30-33, was added later.

8. The same-sex theme and the Philip references were present in Q prior to the creation of *PES*.

How Could We Miss
the Same-Sex Couples in Luke 17?

P eople have missed, refused to see or been able to avoid the presence of gay and lesbian couples in the Couples Material for various reasons. Evidence of the underlying facts of the Galilee Episode is found in references to 1) the warnings about Pharisees, 2) descriptions of raids and entrapment, 3) the denunciation of Bethsaida and Chorazin for the organized rejection, 4) the targeting of gays and lesbians, and 5) the uneven results which resulted from a jurisdictional dispute. There were reasons why each of these aspects of the Galilee Incident escaped our notice.

First, the Pharisees were for many years ignored as agents of persecution for reasons including a) a reaction against their traditional utility as the go-to bad guys for orthodox Christianity, b) the dangers of continued stoking of anti-Judaism, and 3) an apparent lack of evidence of Pharisaic presence in the Galilee.

Second, the entrapment techniques were undetected by Christian commentators and theologians because of the "messianic deceiver" theologizing borrowed from Matthew (where it is) and applied to Luke (where it is not). Christian scatologists simply harmonized the material from Luke and Matthew to form a single, homogenized account. The compulsion to "defend" the Bible against charges of contradiction (which is at present misguided) took priority over the legitimate desire to discern the historical events underlying the gospel accounts.

Third, the location of the incidents, the towns of Bethsaida and Chorazin, have been ignored recently, mainly because there was no existing narrative of events in the two towns that would merit such a denunciation. For some scholars, a single mention is considered too thin a basis for conclusions about the provenance of composition.

Fourth, the gay and lesbian identity of the targeted couples was long missed and later flatly denied. The reasons for this fall into two broad categories, theological and personal, which are closely connected in many primates. People needn't have "latent same-sex attractions" yet feel conflicted about personal sexual conflicts in the past and ongoing temptation. The sexual mores of our numerous primate cousins, from same-sex couplings to rape to polygamy, is both adequate testimony to our genetic inheritance as well as grounds for denial of such relationship. People with same-sex attractions are a convenient scapegoat for two categories of orthodox Christian primates: those untroubled by same-sex attractions, and those who are. The social rejection that these primates experience because they publicly reject homosexuality is to them first, evidence of their basic rightness with God and second, their opposition to sin, even when they fail to experience complete deliverance from sexual sin as individuals.

Finally, the unevenness of results was misinterpreted. Many readers were biased, searching for eschatological, apocalyptic judgment explanations. That is to say, "*God* took one but not the other because..." These interpreters incorrectly assumed that judgment was the theme of Luke 17 and that a deity was the agent of that judgment. Because of these assumptions, Paul's declaration that God made no distinction between Jew and Gentile automatically ruled out ethno-religious explanations such as, "The one seized was a Jew, the one left was a gentile." This is ironic, because such ethno-religious factors were the precise cause of the disparate treatment. Theology can bring us to exactly the wrong understanding of a passage's meaning. As Neusner observed in a different context, "Religious and theological disputes have seriously impeded the study of pre-70 Pharisaism." [154]

Among Christians, one of these theological causes of misinterpretation is the principle of non-contradiction. In one sense this is a problem of logic and philosophy, of sheer words. They feel a compulsion to defend the Bible against the stain of "contradiction." In their minds, contradiction equals error.

In response to criticisms resulting from the inevitable contradictions of multiple supposedly eyewitness accounts, church apologists say having four gospels is a good thing. Having multiple "eyewitness testimonies" to the life and ministry of Jesus is good. On the other hand, these apologists don't value the inevitable tensions and discrepancies. Many people hate that the Bible is such a human document, and they deny the Bible's humanity. They "harmonize" Bible passages instead of accepting that the Bible is a multivocal anthology, that it speaks with many voices.

One illustration of the Bible speaking with multiple voices is found in the story of Jesus driving money changers from the Temple.[155] The synoptic gospels record a single episode of temple cleansing, which appears near the *end* of Jesus' ministry, after his triumphal entry into Jerusalem on a donkey before his crucifixion (Matt. 21:12-13; Mark 11:15-17; Luke 19:45-46). This was apparently the only version of the story until the Gospel of John entered circulation. In John 2:13-16, an expanded version of the episode is placed near the *beginning* of Jesus' ministry, just after the miracle of turning water into wine at the wedding party in Cana. Some conservative Bible interpreters teach that Jesus confronted these exploiters of religious tourists *twice*. Other interpreters explain that the synoptic gospels dramatically illustrate the escalation of tension prior to the crucifixion, while the Johannine gospel employs the scene more theologically.[156]

In the present context, non-contradiction applies primarily to the topic of homosexuality, especially the prohibitions in Leviticus 18:22 and 20:13. On my blog I have discussed those passages and explained why it is theologically illegitimate to invoke the Law as legally binding on non-Jews.[157] I have no problem with acknowledging that differences of human opinion exist in the Bible. Many people of faith have been taught that the Bible must not "contradict" itself. Despite disagreement, I believe that whoever inserted Leviticus 18:22 and 20:13 into the Holiness Code believed that same-sex activity needed to be forbidden. Christian or not, we are under no obligation to agree.

The couples' non-standard sexual orientation has in fact been repeatedly recognized and refuted. Every disavowal of "anything sexual going on" in Luke 17 recognizes the *prima facie* grounds for seeing that the Couples Couplet can refer to sexual activity. This linguistic evidence was the genesis of the present investigation.

Another reason we have missed the sexual orientation of the couples is our expectations, and we've touched on this already. We came to Luke 17 expecting to find eschatology, final judgment. This expectation is rooted in non-contradiction and harmonization. Matthew 24 has a well-developed eschatology, and mentions signs of the second coming, false christs, the works. But eschatology is not referenced here. In Luke, there is no judgment, no grounds for deity doing anything. Indeed, no action is even attributed to deity. There is no justification for introjecting divine judgment into the text of Luke 17, not in the stories of Noah and Lot, not in the stories of the two couples.

We've missed the truth of the Couples Material because of expectations. We came expecting to find prophecy. Our problem? The solution to the biggest puzzle in the passage is historical, not eschatological. Why the disparate treatment regarding the couples, with one person taken, the other left? What does that mean? The passage began as a historical record. There is evidence in Luke of persecution and death, trials before assemblies and magistrates, even the deception used in sting operations. It was recast by ancient scribes in the future tense, as predictive prophecy, but the two-verse fragment is evidence of something problematical.

The knee-jerk compulsion to harmonize kicked in. The reasoning runs something similar to this.

> They can't be homosexuals because all practicing homosexuals are going to hell. There aren't good homosexuals and bad homosexuals. They're in bed, they're grinding—if that means they're having sex, then according to orthodoxy they're all going to hell. They cannot be gay, they cannot be lesbian.

This is the basis for Strauss's criticism, "Perhaps both should have been taken for judgment!" So they can't be having sex in verses 34 and 35. Forget the fact that Lot and Sodom are talked about just a little earlier in verses 28 and 29. Forget that you have sexual content in side-by-side verses 34 and 35. "You only think they're messing around because you've got a dirty mind. Our sex-obsessed culture has made everything about sex. Beds are for sleeping." Let me repeat, as you read the chapter 17, this is the order on the page:

- Lot and Sodom
- at night
- two men in one bed
- one is seized and one is released
- two women grinding together
- one is seized and one is released

Some people miss the same-sex couples because they have only heard the passage discussed as eschatology, referring to the rapture. They long ago lost interest in these topics and have moved on to more pressing human concerns. They are understandably shocked to discover "rapture verses" discussed as evidence that Jesus discussed same-sex couples. I know I was surprised at first, then shocked and briefly appalled. The text we're examining is not about God's apocalyptic judgment.

Some progressive, inclusive, gay-affirming Christians have objected because they've already proven to their satisfaction that Sodom is not about homosexuality, it's about hospitality. So, when Jesus mentions Sodom, he's not talking about gays and lesbians. I've believed for a long time that the Bible is a multivocal book. It speaks with many voices, and these voices are not always in agreement. The legal minds who composed and inserted Leviticus 18:22 and 20:13 likely believed that Genesis 19 was a denunciation of homosexuality (or its idiomatic equivalent). The person who wrote Ezekiel 16:49-50 disagreed with them on the subject and wrote a response. Some people require a non-contradictory sourcebook for their faith. The idea that the Bible contains differences of opinion, an actual conversation, is not something that has come up for them before.

Some gays and lesbians believe that the story of Sodom in no way refers to them. That belief may, in real life, be more important than the fact that Jesus did refer to them. And that's okay. Their mental health and survival really *are* more important than anything I've written. The same holds true for people who believe the term "Christian homosexual" is an oxymoron. Some people's sexual self-control is so tenuous that they cannot contemplate anything but a uniformly rigid standard of behavior applicable for everyone. Allowing a master to judge his own servant does not extend this far. If only this attitude did not contribute to so many suicides.

Evidence of the underlying facts of the Galilee Episode is found in 1) warnings about the Pharisees, 2) the denunciation of Bethsaida and Chorazin for the organized rejection, 3) descriptions of raids and entrapment, 4) the targeting of gays and lesbians, and 5) the uneven results which resulted from a jurisdictional dispute. Each of these aspects of the Galilee Incident escaped notice for specific reasons.

The earliest strata of information testify to this Clean-Up-the-Galilee campaign, which did not necessarily target Jesus followers, but nevertheless did target non-conformist, non-observant Galilean Jews. A Torah-justified campaign such as this was almost certainly waged. Gays and lesbians were slam-dunk convictions for aggressive young prosecutors. People often don't deal well with differences, and in a village or small town these sexual minority, mixed ethnicity couples were convenient targets of opportunity for militant Torah enforcement. Evidence for the Galilee Episode has been preserved in archaeological remains, Josephus, the Talmud and the gospels.

Finally, there is a reason the gay and lesbian presence has been missed in the recent scholarly enterprise. I think some felt that the standard sources (Josephus, Talmud, gospels, etc.) had run dry, that there wasn't enough left to glean from those fields to support the academic mission. Admission requirements for some graduate programs began allowing applicants to substitute statistics training and programming skills for traditional necessities such as German and Latin. The realization that standard historical resources were nearly depleted allowed sociological and economic investigations to enrich the field of New Testament studies. Then, because of this transition, cultural changes enabled some primates to approach historical records differently and acknowledge the presence of sexual minorities in places where they had always been.

Conclusion

What follows is a narrative of the historical episode and its aftermath I have presented here.

Pharisees were individual laymen who occupied a variety of positions in Temple-state government. In a campaign to bring the Galilee region firmly under control of the Jerusalem government, "Bible-believing" Pharisees lead by Yoḥanan b. Zakkai targeted gay and lesbian Jews by means of entrapment and raids. Centuries after the fact, rabbis recorded the entrapment procedures used against ideological opponents. Scribes took no notice of this campaign in the Jewish territories of Archelaus and Antipas. The territory of Philip the Tetrarch, however, contained only a small number of Jews, some in Bathyra, and others living in the far west near the northeast shore of the Sea of Galilee. When Pharisees arrested ethnically mixed gay and lesbian couples in Bethsaida and Chorazin, Philip the Tetrarch ruled judicially on behalf of arrested gentiles, ordering their release from custody. Traces of this jurisdictional conflict are found in Luke, Matthew and the Talmud.

Philip the Tetrarch protected the non-Jewish communities from Jewish legal prosecution, but it was not the agenda of subsequent Christians or Jews to record the "Roman" protection of sexual minorities. Christians and Jews had their separate motives for ignoring the conflict, but details of the campaign's leader and targets survive. An outline of Yoḥanan b. Zakkai can be assembled from the Talmud, and target-relevant details of the campaign are in the gospels. Early Christian scribes were divided over whether to preserve the gay and lesbian identity of the original targets. Later theologians displayed reactionary denial regarding the evidence.

I did not begin this research knowing where it would lead. I simply wondered if there was any evidence that the people in Luke 17:34-35 were gays and lesbians. This question led me to examine the two verses and look for Old Testament antecedents. That evidence included the word *grind*. Next, I investigated the Two-Source hypothesis, and then the Pharisee Yoḥanan b. Zakkai. My search in Josephus began with his descriptions of the Pharisees, and eventually brought me to the least known son of Herod the Great, Philip the Tetrarch. It's amazing what can happens when you tug a single thread.

I have not addressed *how* the gay and lesbian couples are connected to Jesus. But I don't consider it a question of *if* they had connection. Jesus would probably not have discussed the persecution and trials in such detail if he had no personal connection. It seems apparent that Jesus was talking *to* his community *about* his community. Jesus and the compilers of the earliest traditions were sympathetic to the legal and social situation of gays and lesbians, otherwise the references would not have been preserved. The struggle they documented was the struggle of their own community.

I don't know the form of the original Philip materials, those materials consisting of at least the Couples Couplet, the lightning and eagles material, and the Parousia material. I do feel confident that no matter what their original form or purpose, the preservation of the Philip Materials was motivated, that is, references to the couples, their trial, and the nature of Philip's jurisdiction and mode of travel became part of the Q Source for a reason.[158]

At a bare minimum, one of the Q compilers felt that Philip's reign, 1) his judicial fairness in dealing with Jew-gentile relations, 2) his judicial governing style, 3) his philosophy of sojourning among his people, someone felt this was worth preserving, for some reason. The fact of his childlessness and his obscure relationship with Salome his wife were apparently not off-putting to this scribe.

If the Present Thesis is Correct

If the present thesis is correct, then the warning about being taken before magistrates and assemblies (Luke 12:11) almost certainly concerns charges of sodomy, vis-à-vis Leviticus 18:22 and 20:13. If the present thesis is correct, then the warnings about Jesus not bringing peace but a sword, and one's enemies being the members of one's family (Mt 10:34-36; Lk 12:51-53) probably concerned family conflicts engendered by the discovery of differing sexual orientations within families. If the present thesis is correct, then the various gospel discussion of arrest and prosecution, the pre-trial coaching, needs to be correlated with the Galilee Episode. Much of the persecution and trial material discussed here derives from the Pharisaic Galilee reclamation campaign, with a few verses deriving from events in the tetrarchy of Philip, a key figure. If the present thesis is correct, and the Lukan Jesus mentions the Pharisaic prosecution of gays and lesbians and Philip's ruling, the relationship of Jesus to the targeted gay and lesbian community needs continued exploration, as does the relationship between the proposed events of the Galilee Episode and their subsequent theological utility.

I am intrigued by the fact that this previously undiscerned legal ruling (Luke 17:34-35) arose in Bethsaida subsequent to 30 CE in the jurisdiction of Philip the Tetrarch. While his territory doesn't seem to have had a handy name in his lifetime, shortly after his death most of Philip's domain became part of the Roman Province of Arabia. Paul's so-called mystery years in "Arabia" took place, not in what we know as Saudi Arabia, but in this Roman Arabia, which is very close to the road to Damascus, Syria (Gal. 1:17). Arabia was Philip's territory. The trial of the same-sex couples was conducted in the same area as both Paul's Damascus Road Experience and his three year retreat. The place where Jesus followers were first called Christians was nearby Syrian Antioch.

That brings us to the end of this discussion of the Galilee Episode. I've been asking myself the big question, "So what?" Most people on the planet are not Christian and are predominantly heterosexual. Ancient history is precisely that, *ancient*. At a time when the species is facing three predictable and inevitable crises (sea level rise, autonomous artificial intelligence and genetically enhanced primates), how important is a 2,000 years old campaign of territorial consolidation?

On a continuum of genocide that includes Armenia, Cambodia, Native Americans, the Sudan, the Shoah and the monthly police shooting of an unarmed black man, where do you put this domestic police action?

As in so many people's researches, the conclusions I've reached raise so many questions. Why were the law enforcement origins of the Pharisees so widely ignored—or is it just me? Why is it so easy for us (myself included) to dismiss, even rail against, the "social control" function of religious institutions? My main conclusion is that one of the earliest and oldest layers of gospel material testifies to multiple police vice raids, the persecution of gay and lesbian *'am ha-aretz* by Jewish authorities, yet the raids, their anti-homosexual motivation, and the identity of those who conducted them have been expunged or obscured by Judaism and Christendom for 2,000 years.

What does it mean that Christendom possesses evidence of gay and lesbian persecution, evidence that never impugns the character or spirituality of the targets, that the raids are among the foundational events in our gospels, yet the hierarchies bank the benefits paid for with the blood of their own pre-Crucifixion martyrs?

What does it mean that there is arguably evidence in the gospel of the disagreement over the presence of sexual minorities among Jesus followers? What does it mean that one of the central players in the Luke 17 conflict, Philip the Tetrarch, is virtually unknown, with his presence effaced in both Jewish and Christian sources?

What does it mean that the founders of Judaism and Christendom had no use for a narration of the Galilean purification campaign against gay and lesbian couples, but rather expunged and obscured existing evidence and ignored then-living witnesses, with no apparent or likely coordination or consultation?

What seems more reasonable, that a duly qualified Torah enforcement official led a vigorous campaign to purify northwest Palestine of pockets of disobedience to Torah, or that Yoḥanan b. Zakkai, who once joined his comrades in Jerusalem and subsequently founded Rabbinic Judaism in Yavneh, that this sage spent almost twenty years whining in Galilee, pathetic and defeated, rendering only three decisions?

Which of these Scripture-based scenarios seems more likely, that God is going to supernaturally snatch up all true Christians into heaven in bodily form before, during or after the Great Tribulation, or that Torah-enforcing Pharisees targeted sexual transgressors at a time when the Jews were still a self-governing nation, and that tattered, disjointed testimony to this gay and lesbian persecution survived unrecognized?

Takeaways

1. The warning about being taken before magistrates and assemblies (Luke 12:11) may concern charges of sodomy, vis-à-vis Leviticus 18:22 and 20:13.

2. Jesus' comments about not bringing peace but a sword, and one's enemies being the members of one's family (Mt 10:34-36; Lk 12:51-53) likely regard family conflict over sexual orientation.

3. Some, though not necessarily all, of the early gospel discussions of arrest and prosecution and the pre-trial coaching relate to sexual orientation.

Epilogue

The adornment on a 3rd century CE sarcophagus features Ganymede and Zeus. Zeus and Ganymede are the primary same-sex symbols in Roman religion. The Phrygian youth uselessly flails against an empire which feels entitled to disrespect him. Conquered Phrygia vs Imperial Rome. The eagle is the supreme god, Ganymede a mere demigod, yet the beautiful boy is deliberately defaced. A vandal's damage prevents us from seeing the victim's face.

Classicist and photographer Genevra Kornbluth explained how the frame "at the top of the relief and the right edge are made of different material, with a different surface texture, from the figural part." She said that this sort of sarcophagus restoration is "not unusual, as the edges of the stone are always more vulnerable to damage than the center. The top edge of a sarcophagus must often be restored—picture it sticking up out of the ground if the object was mostly buried over time."[159]

Deliberate defacement was common in times of political upheaval. Surviving busts of Roman emperors often have damaged noses. Statues of deities from the Roman pantheon frequently exist with face and pelvis deliberately disfigured. Such defacement was not restricted to antiquity. One incident of vandalism occurred at the cusp of the twentieth century during an excavation of Corinth in Greece.

> The destruction of statues by smashing the nose (or more) is well-known to us. ... [I]n 1901 ... a workman, uncovering a small head of Aphrodite, promptly "battered the head"! This apparently happened "frequently" in early modern Greece.[160]

The vandalism of the same-sex icon on the Hungarian sarcophagus is similar to the vandalism of the same-sex couples in Luke 17, except one is marble and the other is parchment. Each artifact, fortunately, can be restored and recognized.

Photo by Genevra Kornbluth, used by permission.

End Notes

[1] The Greek word *epithumia* (ἐπίθυμία) is generally rendered *lust*. This was apparently an undignified word for clerics to utter during the pulpit reading of the Bible, so for reasons of propriety, to protect young ears from relevant language, a polysyllabic obfuscation was preferred over an anglo saxon gut punch.

[2] This latecomer to the canon appeared in several different locations, in the gospels of both Luke and John. It was a profound and complex tale in search of a good home.

[3] "For there are three that bear record [*in heaven, the Father, the Word, and the Holy Ghost: and these three are one.* [8]*And there are three that bear witness in earth*], the Spirit, and the water, and the blood: and these three agree in one."

[4] Neusner, Jacob. *From Politics to Piety: The Emergence of Pharisaic Judaism*. Prentice-Hall: Englewood Cliffs, NJ, 1973, p 45.

[5] Bickerman 1962, p. 168.

[6] Jacob Neusner (1932-2017), author of over 900 books, taught the theology of Judaism, and history at Bard College.

[7] Neusner, Jacob. *From Politics to Piety: The Emergence of Pharisaic Judaism*. New York, Ktav Publishing House, 1979, 52.

[8] This period is discussed by Elias Bickerman in *From Ezra to the Last of the Maccabees: Foundations of Post-Biblical Judaism*. New York: Schocken Books, 1962, 170; Hanan Eshel in *The Dead Sea Scrolls and the Hasmonean State*. Grand Rapids, MI and Cambridge: Wm. B. Eerdmans, 2008; and Steven Mason in *Josephus' Pharisees: The Philosophy*. Series: Quest of the Historical Pharisees, edited by Jacob Neusner and Bruce D. Chilton. Waco, TX: Baylor UP, 2007, 9-10.

[9] Neusner, *Politics,* 1973, 52.

[10] Murphy, Frederick J. *Early Judaism from the Exile to the Time of Jesus*. Peabody, MA: Hendrickson Publishers, 2002, 289-90.

[11] The so-called Shammaites is the name assigned by Yavnean rabbis to the dominant party of the Pharisees, more militant and confrontational than the Hillelites, the Pharisees who predominated after 70 CE. In the Talmud, the House of Shammai was characterized as consistently opposed to the House of Hillel.

[12] Mason, 2007, p. 12.

[13] Jewish Encyclopedia, 1906.

[14] Closely related to this struggle for freedom from oppression were the activities of Judas' sons, Jacob and Simon. The Jacob and Simon Uprising in the Galilee climaxed between 46 and 48 CE. The Romans again defeated the Jewish forces, suppressing Jewish aspirations for independence. While a record of Judas' crucifixion is strangely absent, Josephus does record the crucifixion of Jacob and Simon, some forty years after the defeat of their messianic father.

[15] Unless otherwise noted, all rabbinic sources regarding 9 Adar are taken from *The Story of the 9th of Adar Told through Disagreements,* by Daniel Roth. http://elmad.pardes.org/wp-content/uploads/2014/01/The-Story-of-9Adar-A-Day-of-Disagreement.pdf.

[16] Hilchot Gedolot, Laws of TishaB'Av (Rabbi Shimon Kayyara, 9th Cen. Babylonia).

[17] Fragment from Land of Israel Prayer Book (pre-9th Century)

[18] Babylonian Talmud, 17a.

[19] Beit = House, Beit Shammai = House of Shammai, or Shammaites.

[20] Neusner, Jacob. *Development of a Legend: Sudies on the Traditions Concerning Yoḥanan b. Zakkai,* Netherlands, Brill, 1970.

[21] Radical skeptics question the value of any Talmudic testimony regarding first-century Palestine. And at the opposite end of the spectrum every word is true. I generally accept the opinions of my guide in these matters, who laid for himself a foundation of desirable historical skepticism with which I feel comfortable.

[22] Neusner, Jacob. *First-Century Judaism in Crisis: Yoḥanan ben Zakkai and the Renaissance of Torah.* Nashville, Abingdon Press, 1971.

[23] "We cannot ignore the fact that whatever we know about Yoḥanan ben Zakkai has been handed on to us by later generations. They recalled what

they *could* believe about him, and they could believe only what made sense in their own situation. People did not keep alive traditions, sayings, or stories because they were antiquarians, but because they thought them holy or important." (Neusner, *Crisis*, p. 192).

[24] Neusner, *Legend*, pp 6-7.

[25] Eagleton, Terry. *Literary Theory: An Introduction*. Oxford: Basil Blackwell, 1983, p 178.

[26] Neusner, Jacob, *From Politics to Piety: The Emergence of Pharisaic Judaism*. Prentice-Hall: Englewood Cliffs, NJ, 1973, pp 2, 44.

[27] One reason for Neusner's reticence is his own corrective mantra for rabbinic Judaism, "What we cannot show, we do not know." If he cannot demonstrate a conviction from sources acceptable to his most important audience, then he refrains from voicing them. But he sure seems to point the way.

[28] Neusner was an iconoclastic academic well acquainted with controversy. Besides his contentious relations, two aspects of his academic product stand out. First is his translation of the Talmud, against which many people railed. Second is his prodigious literary output, which causes even his admirers to shake their heads. Unlike these, his early work on Yoḥanan b. Zakkai is some of his most acclaimed among academics. It seems to be considered spot on by those in a better position to critique him than myself.

[29] Lit., "who will take the dirt from your eyes!"

[30] Mishnah Sotah 5:5b, Jack Abramowitz, trans., https://www.ou.org/torah/gemara/mishna-yomit/sotah_5_4-5/.

[31] Ronald L. Eisenberg, trans. "What the Rabbis Said: 250 Topics from the Talmud." ABC-CLIO, August 3, 2010, Santa Barbara, 2010.

[32] This general task was not restricted to what became rabbinic Judaism. The Apostle Paul was a bicultural Pharisee-rabbi turned missionary-pastor, and this sociopolitical issue (now called Church-and-State) is present in Romans 13:1-6 prior to 70 CE.

[33] Mishnah Sanhedrin 5; trans. Dany, p. 388; quoted in Neusner *Legend*, 51.

[34] 'For no one who has a defect shall approach: a blind man, or a lame man, or he who has a disfigured *face,* or any deformed *limb,* or a man who has a broken foot or broken hand, or a hunchback or a dwarf, or *one who has* a defect in his eye or eczema or scabs or crushed testicles. 'No man among the descendants of Aaron the priest who has a defect is to come near to offer the LORD'S offerings by fire; *since* he has a defect, he shall not come near to offer the food of his God. 'He may eat the food of his God, *both* of the most holy and of the holy, only he shall not go in to the veil or come near the altar because he has a defect, so that he will not profane My sanctuaries. For I am the LORD who sanctifies them.'" So Moses spoke to Aaron and to his sons and to all the sons of Israel.

[35] A summary judgment is a legal ruling that no trial is necessary because circumstances are such that a determination requires no trial.

[36] (Tos Parah 3:8, ed. Zuckermandel, p. 632 ls. 18-22) (Neusner *Legend*, 75).

[37] I read the passage to my Iraqi-American wife, and she recognized it immediately. "My father used to say that to me," she said. "It is a military saying, one who says it has the power."

[38] The Bathyrans were Babylonian Jewish immigrants who came at the time of Herod and were settled in frontier regions, protect the border. They founded the town of Bathyra, whence the name. Herod put some of them into the Temple hierarchy. They next turn up at Yavneh, where they are represented as opposing Yoḥanan b. Zakkai's right to make liturgical decisions formerly vested in the Temple. (Neusner, *Politics* 1973, p. 27).

[39] (b. R.H. 29b) Neusner *Legend*, 93.

[40] "The story of John Hyrcanus's banquet for his Pharisaic clients, his request for critical input, the Pharisaic praise of his reign, except for the discordant note of serious criticism of Hyrcanus and suggestion that he ought not be high priest because of the possible wartime violation of his mother. This is where the Sadducees asked what punishment ought to be administered to Eleazar, 'who had an evil nature and took pleasure in dissension,' according to Josephus." (Saldarini 1988, p. 87)

[41] Neusner, *Legend*, p. 298.

[42] The Talmud's triple attestation corresponds to the Torah's triple attestation for one and the same law for both Jew and non-Jew. "One law

shall be to him that is homeborn, and unto the stranger that sojourneth among you," (Ex 12:49); "Ye shall have one manner of law, as well for the stranger, as for one of your own country: for I *am* the LORD your God," (Lev 24:22); "One law and one manner shall be for you, and for the stranger that sojourneth with you," (Num 15:16).

[43] These excerpts are on pages 129-130 of Neusner's *A Life of Yoḥanan ben Zakkai* (1962).

[44] Neusner, *Life*, 129.

[45] *Rabban*: honorific title posthumously granted to Yoḥanan b. Zakkai which retroactively justifies his speaking and acting in a way that no ordinary mortal would dare.

[46] Neusner, *Life*, p. 223.

[47] Lesson: a Pharisee is under no obligation to volunteer unrequested information. This is still good advice for anyone interviewed for a deposition. Also good advice for anyone facing hostile interrogators in general.

[48] Think: reputation rehabilitation; think: deemphasize the bad precedent of an over-aggressive prosecutor.

[49] Herod Antipas and Philip the Tetrarch are both mentioned in Luke. The gospel of Luke reflects the great effort necessary to insure its account a historical context. Luke 3:1 reads, "Now in the fifteenth year of the reign of Tiberius Caesar, Pontius Pilate being governor of Judaea, and Herod being tetrarch of Galilee, and his brother Philip tetrarch of Ituraea and of the region of Trachonitis, and Lysanias the tetrarch of Abilene." Later, in verse 19 we read, "But Herod the tetrarch, being reproved by him for Herodias his brother Philip's wife, and for all the evils which Herod had done."

[50] Soon after 70 CE Philip's eastern territory would be designated the "Roman Province of Arabia." This "Roman Arabia" is the Arabia where the Apostle Paul spent three years (Gal. 1:17).

[51] The *dorshe hamurot* were a pre-70 Jewish school of interpretation and exegesis which emphasized allegory and symbolism.

[52] Neusner, *Life*, p. 129.

⁵³ Mishnah Sotah 9:9, 15, Danby trans, pp 304-6. Cited in Neusner, *Legend*, p. 50.

⁵⁴ In Acts 29:20 Paul the Apostle is quoted as saying, "I kept back nothing that was profitable *unto you*". Nothing is said here about what would be unprofitable.

⁵⁵ Neusner, *Legend*, 41.

⁵⁶ The Seven Hermeneutic Laws of R. Hillel are as follows:

1. **Ḳal va-ḥomer:** "Argumentum a minori ad majus" or "a majori ad minus"; corresponding to the scholastic proof a fortiori. [lesser to greater reasoning]

2. **Gezerah shavah:** Argument from analogy. Biblical passages containing synonyms or homonyms are subject, however much they differ in other respects, to identical definitions and applications.

3. **Binyan ab mi-katub eḥad:** Application of a provision found in one passage only to passages which are related to the first in content but do not contain the provision in question.

4. **Binyan ab mi-shene ketubim:** The same as the preceding, except that the provision is generalized from two Biblical passages.

5. **Kelal u-Peraṭ and Peraṭ u-kelal:** Definition of the general by the particular, and of the particular by the general.

6. **Ka-yoẓe bo mi-maḳom aḥer:** Similarity in content to another Scriptural passage.

7. **Dabar ha-lamed me-'inyano:** Interpretation deduced from the context.

http://www.jewishencyclopedia.com/view.jsp?artid=472&letter=R]

⁵⁷ For discussions of blood guilt, see
https://www.jewishvirtuallibrary.org/bloodguilt,
https://en.wikipedia.org/wiki/Thou_shalt_not_kill,
https://wol.jw.org/en/wol/d/r1/lp-e/1200000775,
https://www.biblegateway.com/resources/encyclopedia-of-the-bible/Bloodguiltiness-Bloodguilt.

⁵⁸ The Tanaaitic period (also called the Mishaic period) went from approximately 10-220 CE. Neusner believes that the Ribaz material

underwent a brutal pruning process in the decades immediately following his death.

[59] Berakhot 34b.

[60] Neusner, *Legend*, 6,7.

[61] Neusner, *Crisis*, 193-4.

[62] Hengel, Martin. *Acts and the History of Earliest Christianity*. London, SCM Press, Ltd. 1979. p. 76.

[63] Sim, David C. "How Many Jews became Christians in the First Century? The Failure of the Christian Mission to the Jews." HTS, 2005, p. 429.

[64] In police dramas such "turf disputes" often occur when local detectives are in conflict with law enforcement agencies higher on the food chain, like state investigators or the FBI. When considering an army of occupation, however, such comparisons are useful, but imprecise.

[65] Lefkowitz, Rabbi Philip. "Judah Macabee – Homophobe" (n.d.), *Unorthodox Orthodoxy*, http://www.agudasachimnsc.org/articles/index.html?macabee.html.

[66] Robert Lowth's *Lectures on the Sacred Poetry of the Hebrews* was printed in 1787, and originally published in Latin as *De sacra poesi Hebraeorum* in 1753 (Encyclopedia Britannica, https://www.britannica.com/biography/Robert-Lowth).

[67] If you search for the word "bed" in an English translation of the two Leviticus verses, you will not find it, since translators have translated the idiom into intelligible English. Literally, Leviticus 18:22 would read, "*and with male not-you-shall-lie-down beds-of woman abhorrence she,*" and Leviticus 20:13 would read, "*and man who he is lying down with beds-of woman abhorrence they-did two-of-them to-be-put-to-death they-shall-be-put-to-death bloods-of-them in-them.*"

[68] Many religious supporters of LGBT folks make difficult Biblical arguments, many of which involve word meanings. I make such arguments myself. There are places, as in these Levitical prohibitions, where I don't dispute the usual rendering. While I have studied Biblical Hebrew, I don't count myself an expert.

[69] Like other languages, Hebrew has many expressions for sexual intercourse. "To lie with," "to know," "to uncover someone's nakedness"—just a few Hebrew idioms for sex.

[70] Shoulson, Jeffrey, Milton and the Rabbis: Hebraism, Hellenism, and Christianity. Yale UP, 2001, 254. See also Susan Niditch, *Judges: A Commentary*, Westminster John Knox Press, 2008, p 171, and "Eroticism and Death in the Tale of Jael," in *Gender and Difference in Ancient Israel*, ed. Peggy Lynne Day, Fortress Press, 1989, p 48.

[71] See Maria Eriksson Baaz & Maria Stern (2018) "Curious erasures: the sexual in wartime sexual violence," *International Feminist Journal of Politics*, 20:3, 295-314, DOI: 10.1080/14616742.2018.1459197.

[72] For discussions of Contemporary Wartime Male Rape, see Archer, John and Barbara Lloyd, *Sex and Gender*, Cambridge: Cambridge UP, 2002, p 129; Donnan, Hastings and Fiona Magowan, *The Anthropology of Sex*, London: Berg Publishers, 2010, p 147; Scarce, Michael. *Male on Male Rape: The Hidden Toll of Stigma and Shame*. New York: Perseus Publishing, 2008, p. 47; and Shigematsu, Setsu and Keith L. Comacho, eds. *Militarized Currents: Toward a Decolonized Future in Asia and the Pacific*, Minneapolis: U of Minnesota Press, 2010, p. 227.

For discussions of Ancient Wartime Male Rape, see Carden, Michael, *Sodomy: A History of a Christian Biblical Myth,* London, Equinox Publishing Ltd., 2004, p 35; Gelb, Joyce and Marian Lief Palley, *Women and Politics Around the World: A Comparative History and Survey*, Volume 1, ABC-CLIO, Santa Barbara, CA, 2009, p. 107; Goldstein, Joshua S., *War and Gender: How Gender Shapes the War System and Vice Versa*, Cambridge UP, 2010, p. 359; Petrak, Jenny and Barbara Hedge, *The Trauma of Sexual Assault: Treatment, Prevention and Practice*, John Wiley & Sons, 2003, p. 3.

For discussions of Wartime Child Rape, see Horvitz, Leslie Alan, and Christopher Catherwood, *Encyclopedia of War Crimes and Genocide*, New York: Facts on File, 2006, p. 77; Hyder Tina Hyder *War, Conflict and Play*, Series, Debating Play, Series ed. Tina Bruce Open University Press, Berkshire, UK, 2004, p. 8; Parrot, Andrea and Nina Cummings, *Forsaken Females: The Global Brutalization of Women*, Rowman & Littlefield, Lanham, MD, 2006, p. 100; Sheldon, Kathleen E. *Historical*

Dictionary of Women in Sub-Saharan Africa, Scarecrow Press, Lanham, MD, 2005, p. 211.

[73] Halloran, John A. *Sumerian Lexicon, Version 3.0.* https://www.sumerian.org/sumcv.htm.

[74] "The verb *permolere* (to grind grain) is an agricultural term transferred to a sexual context; cf. Adams 1982 (152-53)." N. 4, p 95, *Sexuality in Greek and Roman Society and Literature: A Sourcebook,* Marguerite Johnson and Terry Ryan, London: Routledge, 2005.

[75] Kiefer, Otto, Gilbert and Helen Highet, trans. Sexual Life in Ancient Rome. London, New York, Routledge, 2012, p. 66.

[76] Pittacus (c. 640 – 568 BCE), ancient Mytilenaen military general; one of the Seven Sages of Greece.

[77] For a discussion of work songs, see Norm Cohen, *Folk Music: A Regional Exploration*, Santa Barbara, CA, Greenwood, 2005, p. 32.

[78] Magill, Frank Northen, *Dictionary of World Biography*, London, Salem Press, 1998, p. 860.

[79] The Greek words in Luke and Plutarch are different forms of the same root αλη (*grind*). The word in Luke is αληθουσαι. The word in Plutarch is αλη.

[80] One must tread cautiously. In English, the word *groovy* (excellent) is found in 1937, and *gams* (legs) was recorded in 1781, over 80 and 230 years ago respectively. Our use of the words *slang, idiom, vulgar* and *euphemism* can be imprecise and rhetorical.

[81] In the Japanese Kamasutra there are no less than eleven sexual uses of *grinding* using the phrase "tea-grinding mill" or "tea-grinding hand mill"

Raft-style Tea-grinding Mill (いかだ様式の茶粉砕の製造所),
Weaving Tea-grinding Hand Mill (編む茶粉砕手),
Drizzling Tea-grinding Mill (小雨が降る茶粉砕の製造所),
Stretched Tea-grinding Mill (伸ばされた茶粉砕の製造所),
Authentic Tea-grinding Mill (確実な茶粉砕の製造所),
Sailboat Tea-grinding Mill (ヨットの茶粉砕の製造所),
Mirrored Tea-grinding Mill (映された茶粉砕の製造所),
Moon-viewing Tea-grinding Mill (月観覧の茶粉砕の製造所),
Cuddled Tea-grinding Mill (抱きしめられた茶粉砕の製造所),

Restrained Tea-grinding Mill (抑制された茶粉砕の製造所), and
Reversed Tea-grinding Mill (逆転させた茶粉砕の製造所).

[82] The Swahili term for lesbians is *wasaga*, which literally means "one who grinds." The word *sagana* is the word for lesbian lovemaking, means "grind together," referring, for example, to lesbian lovemaking in Tanzania. The Swahili words for lesbian(s) are *msagaji* (grinder sing.) and *wasagaji* (plur.), and *msago* (grinder sing.) and *misago* (plur), (Drescher, Jack and Vittorio Lingiardi. *The Mental Health Professions and Homosexuality: International Perspectives*, New York: CRC Press, 2003).

[83] In Chinese the phrase "mirror grinding" (*mojingzi*) is used to describe lesbian sexual behavior. The phrase "mirror grinders" (*mojingzhe*) refers to lesbians. In the late nineteenth century, a lesbian organization called the "Rubbing Mirrors Party" (*Mojing Dang*) was active in Shanghai. Another lesbian activity is called "grinding bean curd." (Topley, Marjorie. *Cantonese Society in Hong Kong and Singapore: Gender, Religion, Medicine and Money; Essays by Marjorie Topley*)

[84] Hokkien is one of the world's largest Chinese dialect groups. Bôa (磨) - literally 'to rub' or 'to grind' is idiomatic for 'having sex,' the imagery being two bodies rubbing against each other. (Wikipedia: Hokkien Profanity)

[85] "In Arabic, the word " سحاقية (siHaaqiyyah) means lesbian. It is derived from the root s7q (one of its meanings is to grind)." "The grinding of saffron (Sahq Al-Za'faran) was once quite a common euphemism for female homosexual activity. Indeed, the Arabic word for lesbian, Suhaqiya, can be transliterated as "grinder." The euphemism originates from medieval Arabic literature, appearing in various texts as early as the ninth century. The word المساحقة comes from the root س-ح-ق, which has, among other meanings, to do with grinding or rubbing, as previously mentioned. Applied to lesbians it probably refers to a certain sexual practice. A more accurate translation for the term might be 'tribadism' or 'tribady', but of course, by extension, lesbianism in general." Samar Habib. *Female Homosexuality in the Middle East: Histories and Representations*, New York: Routledge, 2007.

[86] The German word "*Mahlen*," "to mill, to grind" is an antique metaphor for sexual intercourse." (Youens, Susan. *Schubert, Müller, and Die Schöne Müllerin*, Cambridge: Cambridge UP, 2006. p. 82)

[87] Habib, *ibid.*

[88] The Arabic word for grind is used throughout medieval Arabic in discussions of female lovemaking. *Medieval Arabic 800-1750 An Appendix of Texts from the Arabian Middle Ages Concerned with Female Homosexuality*, Translated from Arabic by Samar Habib. Retrieved 1/3/2012. arts.brunel.ac.uk/gate/entertext/7_2/ET72HabibtransEDrevs .doc

[89] The Tocharian language was discovered in the mid-twentieth century in central Asia. It was spoken from about 300 – 900 CE. It is divided into Tocharian A (the religious form), and Tocharian B (the administrative form). The Tocharian word *yäks* means to "embrace, entangle," referring to the "embrace of lovers." "The obvious derivatives *yäks rye* and *yakso* 'meal, flour' suggest that it may have meant 'squeeze, press (as by a millstone)' as well. It may be, since deverbative nouns in *–iye* are typically formed to Class IV subjunctives (e.g. *lalyiye*, *akalye*, and *ysiye*, qq.v.), that *yäksiye* is derived from a second, otherwise unattested *yäks-* 'grind, mill' that was synchronically distinct but etymologically related to attested *yäks-* 'embrace, entangle.' (Adams, Douglas Q., *A Dictionary of Tocharian B*, Amsterdam-Atlanta, GA, Rodopi, 1999. pp 495-6)

[90] The sexual implications of the word *grind* are highlighted in a discussion of two Oxford students in Chaucer's *The Reeve's Tale* A Companion to Old and Middle English Literature.

[91] The character Pandarus uses *grinding* sexually in the opening scene of Shakespeare's *The History of Troilus and Cressida.*

[92] Gordon Williams documents the sexual use of *grind* in English literature from the sixteenth century to the eighteenth: Buckley (c 1564), Valenger (c 1572), Furnivall (c 1650), Dodsley (1662), *Whore's Rhetorick* (1683), Wade (1673), Ward (1707), Burns, Woodfall, Ebsworth (ca. 1697), Dekker (1611-12), and Cleland (1748) (Williams, Gordon. *A Dictionary of Sexual Language and Imagery in Shakespearean and Stuart Literature.* London: Atlantic Highlands, N.J.: Athlone Press, 1994).

[93] Simons, Patricia. *The Sex of Men in Premodern Europe: A Cultural History*, p 275. Cambridge, UK; New York: Cambridge UP, 2011.

[94] If you were literate in the first century CE, you might have known two or three languages. A literate Roman might have known only Latin, just

as "literate" Americans sometimes know only American English. People in the U.S. who speak only English are at a disadvantage when it comes to new-hires who are required to be bilingual, speaking not only English but Spanish, Arabic, or Chinese, depending on the region. In the age of NAFTA, much of our packaging needs to be printed in English, Spanish, and French.

[95] This from United Methodist pastor John Meunier. "Luke's Gay Apocalypse: Two Lesbians without a Mill," *Formerly the Bible-Thumping Liberal*, https://biblethumpingliberal.com/2011/05/24/the-q-apocalypse-two-lesbians-without-a-mill.

[96] The objective, analytical approach to studying the Bible has only been in widespread practice for the last 500 years or so. Various goals, like *not* highlighting tensions and contradictions in the text, prevented us from analyzing the texts objectively. That is not to say, for example, that the early church fathers were not as objective and analytical as possible. But their use of the text, their goals, differed from later generations.

[97] Ezekiel 16:49-50 says the sin of Sodom was arrogance, overeating, lack of concern for the poor and needy, haughtiness and doing detestable things.

[98] Two instances of entrapment can be found in *Xenophon and the Muleteer: Hubris, Retaliation, and the Purposes of Shame,* David D. Phillips, University of California, Los Angeles (phillips@history.ucla.edu), Colloquium Atticum II, Universität Hamburg, June 20, 2013.

[99] Not to be confused with the Philadelphia of Revelation 3:7-13, which is in present-day Turkey.

[100] Note similar Torah passages. "One ordinance shall be both for you of the congregation, and also for the stranger that sojourneth among you, an ordinance forever in your generations: as ye are, so shall the stranger be before the Lord" (Num 15:15). "And I charged your judges at that time, saying, Hear *the causes* between your brethren, and judge righteously between *every* man and his brother, and the stranger *that is* with him" (Dt 1:16). "Thou shalt not pervert the judgment of the stranger, *nor* of the fatherless; nor take a widow's raiment to pledge" (Dt 27:19).

[101] Archaeological evidence of a sustained Galilee campaign includes 1) the disappearance of ESA, a fine red pottery known as Phoenician

Eastern Sigillata A, 2) the appearance of ritual indoor pools or baths, and 3) the distribution and contents of coin hoards .

[102] The section containing this evidence is quite narrow, not at all like taking verses from Deuteronomy, Psalms and Jude, putting them together and announcing a doctrine. My evidence is from what is sometimes called the Q Source, which is simply all the material which Luke and Matthew share in common apart from Mark. This means, by definition, that the Q source evidence is doubly attested. This "double attestation" factor is worthy of note because it was often argued that such multiple attestation was a sign of reliability.

[103] Oakman, Douglas E. *The Political Aims of Jesus.* Minneapolis, MN: Fortress Press, 2012.

[104] "Anatomy of a Sting Operation" The Process:

"The first phase of a sting operation is identifying a person who poses a potential threat. Leads may come from an informant, a member of the community or even close family. In many cases, the subject will make inflammatory or threatening statements on social media, or they may even have reached out to a known terrorist entity. If the individual is deemed a potential threat, the law enforcement body conducting the operation may choose to proceed with a preliminary inquiry.

"Should this preliminary inquiry indicate that the individual in question does indeed pose a threat, the authorities will open a formal investigation utilizing more resources. Investigators assigned to the case will also begin discussing the matter at hand with a prosecutor who, in the United States, would most likely be an assistant U.S. attorney. The involvement of a legal professional ensures that the operation is conducted lawfully and avoids entrapment while guaranteeing that the criteria required to successfully take the case to trial are met."

[105] Sting operation elements can be located in various places online. https://www.politieacademie.nl/kennisenonderzoek/kennis/mediatheek/P DF/88313.PDF; http://theipti.org/wp-content/uploads/ 2012/02/Toolkit_ ENG_screen.pdf; and Stratfor Enterprises, LLC. "Anatomy of a Sting Operation." Apr 16, 2015. https://worldview.stratfor.com/article/ anatomy-sting-operation. Retrieved 9-18-2018.

[106] Stratfor Enterprises, LLC. "Anatomy of a Sting Operation." April 16, 2015. https://worldview.stratfor.com/article/anatomy-sting-operation.

Accessed 9-20-2018. See also, https://www.politieacademie.nl/
kennisenonderzoek/kennis/mediatheek/PDF/88313.PDF, and http://thei
pti.org/wp-content/uploads/ 2012/02/Toolkit_ENG_screen.pdf.

[107] Concerned traditionalists and dispensationalists are quite experienced
at dismissing interpretive disagreements based on historical events, so I
harbor no illusions that many will be moved to doubt their particular
belief system once for all delivered to the saints, no matter how recent
the vintage.

[108] Tosefta Sanhedrin.

[109] The following text and headings are taken from "*Q: The Lost Sayings
Source: Burton Mack's translation*," https://www.tonyburke.ca/wp-
content/uploads/Burton-Macks-Q-Text.pdf. The passage contains 27
verses, with "Pronouncements Against the Pharisees" (QS 34)
comprising the longest section (13 verses), "On Speaking Out" (QS 35)
has 2 verses, "On Fear" (QS 36) 4 verses, and "On Public Confessions"
(QS 37) has 5.

[110] In this series, QS34 is the longest, and was most subject to expansion
and accretion.

> "Shame*ful* [on you] Pharisees! for you are scrupulous about giving a
> tithe of mint and dill and cumin to the priests, but you neglect justice
> and the love of God."

> "These things you ought to have done, without neglecting the
> others."

> "Shame*ful* [on you] Pharisees! for you clean the outside of the cup
> and the dish, but inside are full of greed and incontinence. Foolish
> Pharisees! Clean the inside and the outside will also be clean."

> "Shame*ful* [on you] Pharisees! for you love the front seats in the
> assemblies and greetings in the marketplaces. Shame*ful* [on you]! for
> you are like graves, outwardly beautiful, but full of pollution inside."

> "Shame*ful* [on you] lawyers! for you load people with burdens heavy
> to bear, but you yourselves refuse to carry even a light load."

> "Shame*ful* [on you]! for you erect memorials for the prophets, the
> prophets your fathers killed. Thus you witness and consent to the
> deeds of your fathers; for they killed the prophets and you build
> monuments to them."

"For this reason the wisdom of God said, 'I will send them prophets and wise men, some of whom they will kill and prosecute,' in order to hold this generation accountable for the blood of all the prophets shed from the foundation of the world, from the blood of Abel to the blood of Zechariah who perished between the altar and the sanctuary. Truly, I tell you, this generation will be held accountable."

"Shame*ful* [on you] lawyers! for you have taken the key of knowledge away from the people. You yourselves do not enter the kingdom of God, and you prevent those who would enter from going in."

[111] https://www.esurance.com/info/car/how-to-handle-a-car-accident.

[112] https://www.washingtonpeacecenter.org/riskarrest.

[113] http://www.actupny.org/documents/CDdocuments/ACTUP_Civil Disobedience.pdf.

[114] My thanks to Andrew Welch for this suggestion.

[115] "Springtime In Iran Means The 'Morality Police' Are Out In Force." https://www.npr.org/sections/parallels/2016/05/03/476511439/springtime -in-iran-means-the-morality-police-are-out-in-force

[116] "Who are Islamic 'morality police'?" https://www.bbc.com/news/ world-middle-east-36101150

[117] "More than 40,000 public order cases annually in Sudan capital," *Dabanga*, https://www.dabangasudan.org/en/all-news/article/more-than-40-000-public-order-cases-annually-in-sudan-capital-sdfg.

[118] In this situation, the accreted material, the distractors, often attracts more attention than what is possibly the historical core of the pericope. So the definition of blaspheming the Holy Spirit eclipses the actual synagogue trial. What could be more important to your salvation than knowing about the unforgiveable sin?

[119] Attorney General Jeff Sessions.

[120] "Chicago Police Superintendent: Criminals think Chicago's Judicial System a Joke," *American Thinker*, February 2018. https://www.americanthinker.com/blog/2018/02/chicago_police_superint endent_criminals_think_chicagos_judicial_system_a_joke.html. Accessed 20.1.2018.

[121] Adapted from contemporary fishing practice, "catch and release" has been adapted, and often refers to the INS policy of releasing unauthorized immigrants while they await immigration hearings, avoiding the cost of keeping them in custody. As a law-and-order slogan, it has replaced "soft on crime" and "coddling criminals." One variant is "trap-and-release."

[122] In "Changing the Subject: Rabbinic Legal Process in the Absence of Justification," Jordan D. Rosenblum discusses Talmud cases "in which a rabbi, faced with a contradictory or complex argument, changes the subject rather than his reasoning or ruling. Through a discussion of such cases, this essay argues that, while not preferable, changing the subject can in fact be a valid rabbinic legal process."

[123] See Anna Carron, "Notes and Comments: Marriage-Based Immigration for Same-Sex Couples after DOMA: Lingering Problems of Proof and Prejudice," Scholarly Commons, Vol. 109, No. 4, https://scholarlycommons.law.northwestern.edu/cgi/viewcontent.cgi?article=1218&context=nulr. Also, Sharita Gruberg, "What the DOMA Decision Means for LGBT Binational Couples," Center for American Progress, June 26, 2013, https://www.americanprogress.org/issues/immigration/news/2013/06/26/68033/what-the-doma-decision-means-for-lgbt-binational-couples/

[124] Strickert, Fred, 1995.

[125] "The Cod Wars" 1958-1976, Britain and Iceland, https://british seafishing.co.uk/the-cod-wars/

"The Cherbourg Dispute" 1993 Britain and France, https://britishseafishing.co.uk/the-cherbourGodispute/

Pitcher, T.J. & Lam, M.E. Maritime Studies (2015) 14: 2. https://doi.org/10.1186/s40152-014-0014-5

[126] Today law enforcement must follow procedures to ensure that evidence will stand up in court. In the contemporary context, the use of tape recordings is governed by "predicate rules" which instruct investigators regarding the foundation they must establish to ensure the evidence is reliable.

[127] Berkowitz, Beth A. *Execution and Invention: Death Penalty Discourse in Early Rabbinic and Christian Cultures*. Oxford: Oxford UP, 2006, pp 14-15.

[128] Neusner, *Legend*, 63.

[129] Neusner, *Crisis*, 192.

[130] Hezser, Catherine, *The Social Structure of the Rabbinic Movement in Roman Palestine*, Mohr Siebeck, Tübingen, 1997, 12-13.

[131] Neusner, *Crisis*, 192.

[132] "These persons are rightly judged worthy of death by those who obey the law, which ordains that the man-woman who debases the sterling coin of nature should perish unavenged, suffered not to live for a day or even an hour, as a disgrace to himself, his house, his native land and the whole human race. And the lover of such may be assured that he is subject to the same penalty." — Philo, Volume VII, edited by G. P. Gould, The Loeb Classical Library (LCL 320), Page 499, year 1998. Quoted by Mare Pacificum Publishing, "Philo on Homosexuality." https://marepacificumpublishing.com/2013/04/14/philo-on-homosexuality/ Retrieved 9/16/2018.

[133] *'Am ha-aretz*, means "people of the land," and was commonly a term of derision, with connotations of rustic, boorish, uncivilized, and ignorant.

[134] This is an unargued assumption.

[135] Neusner, *Crisis*, 193-94.

[136] Neusner, *Crisis*, 52.

[137] Neusner, *Life*, 55.

[138] There is an interesting parallel here, between the couple Solomon and Cleopatra and the couple Philip the Tetrarch and Salome, which I would be loath to ignore but do not unexplore.

[139] Frank J. Matera, *New Testament Theology: Exploring Diversity and Unity*. WJKP, 2007. p 92.

[140] In Matthew, the lightning and the eagles appear together, leading Q scholars to conclude that, in this unusual case, Matthew's arrangement is probably original to Q.

[141] *The Sayings Gospel Q in English Translation*, Minneapolis, MN, Fortress Press, 2001.

[142] The word *Lukan* refers to anything related to the writing of the canonical book of Luke. Thus, we may discuss Lukan scribes, Lukan themes, Lukan tendencies, Lukan community, etc.

[143] If you are not familiar with the Q Hypothesis, let me direct you to three Wikipedia articles: Synoptic Gospels, Two-Source Hypothesis, and Q Source. In a nutshell, two written sources, Mark and Q, were sources used by Matthew and Luke when they wrote their gospels.

[144] Jennings, Theodore W., Jr. and Tat-Siong Benny Liew. "Mistaken Identities but Model Faith: Rereading the Centurion, the Chap, and the Christ in Matthew 8:5-13." *Journal of Biblical Literature. 123/3 (2004) 467–494.*

[145] "I Solomon said unto him: 'Beelzeboul, what is thy employment?' And he answered me: "I destroy kings. I ally myself with foreign tyrants. And my own demons I set on to men, in order that the latter may believe in them and be lost. And the chosen servants of God, priests and faithful men, I excite unto desires for wicked sins, and evil heresies, and lawless deeds; and they obey me, and I bear them on to destruction. And I inspire men with envy, and [desire for] murder, and for wars and sodomy, and other evil things. And I will destroy the world." *The Testament of Solomon*, translated by F. C. Conybeare.

[146] *The Sayings Gospel Q in English Translation*, Minneapolis, MN, Fortress Press, 2001.

[147] The "Lukan authorship" refers to all the scribes who contributed to the creation of canonical Luke after Q was in "general circulation."

[148] For clarity, canonical Luke first appeared without verse 36, "Two men will be in a field, one shall be taken, the other left." Before being circulated the word *field* in verse 34 had been changed to *bed*. Then, a couple of hundred years later, some scribes added the verse again as verse 36.

[149] John S. Kloppenborg, "Q, Bethsaida, Khorazin, and Capernaum," *Q in Context II: Social Setting and Archaeological Background of the Sayings Source*, edited by Markus Tiwald, Göttingen, Vandenhoeck & Ruprecht, 2015, p 6-68.

[150] In Greek that would be "ἡμέραι... ἡμέρᾳ... ἡμέραις... ἡμέραις... ἡμέρας... ἡμέραις... ἡμέρᾳ... ἡμέρᾳ... ἡμέρᾳ... νυκτὶ..."

[151] Perform a word search and you will find nearly 2,500 instances of the phrase *eiusdem sexus.*

[152] Kloppenborg, 1987, 161-2.

[153] "Parousia," *The International Bible Encyclopedia,* Delmarva Publications, 2014.

[154] Neusner, 1973, p 5.

[155] Another example of multiple versions and conflicting edits is the story of "The Anointing of Jesus" Matthew 26, Mark 14, Luke 7, and John 12.

[156] The Temple Cleansing episode does not appear in Q.

[157] Goetz, Ronald. "You Can't Quote Leviticus to Prove God Hates Homosexuality." *Bible Thumping Liberal,* 5/19/2011. https://biblethumpingliberal.com/2011/05/19/you-can%e2%80%99t-quote-leviticus-to-prove-god-hates-homosexuality/

[158] I will say once more, you don't have to subscribe to the entire Two-Source Hypothesis, or Q Hypothesis, to recognize, for example, that the gospel of Luke was produced by historians who depended on documents for composition.

[159] Genevra Kornbluth, email 2/16/2019.

[160] Roger Pearse, "Broken noses, crosses on the forehead – the fate of statues at the end of antiquity," Roger Pearse: Thoughts on Antiquity, Patristics, Information Access and More, July 27, 2018, https://www.roger-pearse.com/weblog/2018/07/27/broken-noses-crosses-on-the-forehead-the-fate-of-statues-at-the-end-of-antiquity/. See also, Amelia R. Brown, "Crosses, noses, walls and wells: Christianity and the fate of sculpture in late antique Corinth," in Troels M. Kristensen, Lea Stirling (eds.), *The Afterlife in Greek and Roman Sculpture: Late Antique Responses and Practices,* U of Michigan, 2016, pp 150, 151.

Bibliography Works Cited

Adams, Douglas Q. *A Dictionary of Tocharian B*. Amsterdam-Atlanta, GA, Rodopi, 1999.

Allison, Jr. Dale C. "The Allusive Jesus." *The Historical Jesus in Recent Research*," (pp. 238-247) Winona Lake, IN: Eisenbrauns, 2005.

--- *The Jesus Tradition in Q*. Harrisburg, PA. Trinity Press International, 1997.

Arnal, William E. *Jesus and the Village Scribes: Galilean Conflicts and the Setting of Q*. Minneapolis: Fortress Press, 2001.

Berkowitz, Beth A. *Execution and Invention: Death Penalty Discourse in Early Rabbinic and Christian Cultures*. Oxford: Oxford UP, 2006.

Bickerman, Elias. *From Ezra to the Last of the Maccabees: Foundations of Post-Biblical Judaism*. New York: Schocken Books, 1962.

Bowman, Alan K. and Greg Woolf, eds. *Literacy and Power in the Ancient World*. Cambridge U.K., Cambridge U.K., 1994.

Bowyer, William. *Critical conjectures and observations on the New Testament: collected from various authors, as well in regard to words as pointing, with the reasons on which both are founded*. London: John Nichols and Sons, 1812.

Burge, Gary M., Lynn H. Cohick, Gene L. Green, *The New Testament in Antiquity: A Survey of the New Testament in its Cultural Context*, Grand Rapids, Zondervan, 2009.

Corely, Kathleen E. *Maranatha: Women's Funerary Rituals and Christian Origins*. Minneapolis: Fortress Press, 2010

Cotter, Wendy. *The Christ of the Miracle Stories: Portrait through Encounters*. Grand Rapids, MI: Baker Academic, 2010.

Crompton, Louis. *Homosexuality & Civilization*. Cambridge: Harvard UP, 2006.

Drescher, Jack and Vittorio Lingiardi. *The Mental Health Professions and Homosexuality: International Perspectives*, New York: CRC Press, 2003

Dunn, James D.G. and Scot McKnight, eds. *The Historical Jesus in Recent Research*. Winona Lake, IN: Eisenbrauns, 2005.

Dynes, Wayne R. and Stephen Donaldson, eds. *Homosexuality In the Ancient World.* New York and London: Garland Publishing, 1992.

Eagleton, Terry. *Literary Theory: An Introduction*. Oxford: Basil Blackwell, 1983.

Edwards, Douglas R. and C. Thomas McCollough, eds. *The Archaeology of Difference: Gender, Ethnicity, Class and the "Other" in Antiquity: Studies in Honor of Eric B. Meyers*. Boston, MA: American Schools of Orient Research, 2007.

Eshel, Hanan. *The Dead Sea Scrolls and the Hasmonean State*. Grand Rapids, MI and Cambridge: Wm. B. Eerdmans, 2008.

Faulkner, Gimel. *The Homeric Hymn to Aphrodite: Introduction, Text, and Commentary*. Oxford: Oxford UP, 2008.

Fellows, Will. *A Passion to Preserve: Gay Men as Keepers of Culture*. Madison, WI: University of Wisconsin Press, 2004.

Fisher, Moshe, ed. *Yavneh, Yavneh-Yam and Their Neighborhood: Studies in the Archaeology and History of the Judea Coastal Plain*. Tel Aviv: Eretz, 2005.

Fleddermann, H.T. *Q: A Reconstruction and Commentary*. Leuven, Paris, Dudley, MA: Peeters, 2005. BiTS (Biblical Tools and Studies, vol. 1), ed. By B. Doyle, G. Van Belle, J. Verheyden, K.U. Leuven.

Fone, Byrne R.S. *Anthology of Gay Literature*. Columbia UP, 1998.

--- *Homophobia: A History.* New York: Macmillan, 2001.

Gambetti, Sandra. *The Alexandrian Riots of 38 C.E. and the Persecution of the Jews: A Historical Reconstruction. Supplements to the Journal for the Study of Judaism 135. Leiden/Boston*: Brill, 2009.

Goodenough, Erwin Ramsdell. *The Jurisprudence of the Jewish Courts in Egypt: Legal Administration by the Jews under the Early Roman Empire as Described by Philo Judaeus.* Yale UP, 1929.

Gramick, Jeannine. *Homosexuality and the Catholic Church.* Chicago: Thomas More Press, 1983.

Habib, Samar. *Female Homosexuality in the Middle East: Histories and Representations.* New York: Routledge, 2012.

--- *Middle Ages Concerned with Female Homosexuality.* Amherst, NY: Teneo Press, 2009.

Haines-Eitzen, Kim. *Guardians of Letters: Literacy, Power, and the Transmitters of Early Christian Literature.* Oxford U.K. and New York: Oxford UP. 2000.

Hallmark, Rufus, ed. *German Lieder in the Nineteenth Century.* Routledge Studies in Musical Genres. 1996.

Halloran, John A. *Sumerian Lexicon, Version 3.0.* PDF. https://is.muni.cz/el/1421/jaro2013/PAPVB_13/um/40794229/Halloran_version_3.pdf.

Han, Kyu Sam. *Jerusalem and the Early Jesus Movement: The Q Community's Attitude Toward the Temple.* London & New York: Sheffield Academic Press, 2002. Journal for the Study of the New Testament. Supplement Series 207.

Harding, James and Alexander Loveday. "Dating the Testament of Solomon," University of St. Gimels: Old Testament Pseudepigrapha, 1999.

Harding, Mark and Alanna Nobbs. *The Content and Setting of the Gospel Tradition.* Grand Rapids, MI and Cambridge U.K.: Wm. B. Eerdmans Publishing Co., 2010.

Hezser, Catherine, *The Social Structure of the Rabbinic Movement in Roman Palestine*, Texte und Studien zum Antiken Judentum 66, Mohr Siebeck, Tübingen, 1997.

Hoenig, Sidney Benjamin. *The Great Sanhedrin: A Study of the Origin, Composition, and Function of the Bet Din ha-Gadol during the Second Jewish Commonwealth.* Philadelphia: Dropsie College for Hebrew and Cognate Learning, 1953.

Horsley, Richard A. "Abandoning the Unhistorical Quest for an Apolitical Jesus." *The Historical Jesus in Recent Research*," (pp. 288-301) Winona Lake, IN: Eisenbrauns, 2005.

--- *Galilee: History, Politics, People.* Valley Forge, PA: Trinity Press International, 1995.

--- Scribes, *Visionaries, and the Politics of Second Temple Judea.* Louisville, London: Westminster John Knox Press, 2007.

Horsley, Richard A. and Jonathan A. Draper. *He Who Hears You Hears Me: Prophets, Performance, and Tradition in Q.* Harrisburg, PA: Trinity Press International, 1999.

Jacobson, Arland D. *The First Gospel: An Introduction to Q.* Sonoma, CA: Polebridge Press, 1992. (Foundations and Facets. Reference Series.

Johnson, Marguerite, and Terry Ryan. *Sexuality in Greek and Roman Society and Literature: A Sourcebook.* London: Routledge, 2005.

Kalmin, Richard. "Talmudic Portrayals of Relationships between Rabbis: Amoraic or Pseudepigraphic?" *Association for Jewish Studies Review.* Vol. 17, No. 2. (Autumn, 1992), pp. 165-197. Stable URL: http://links.jstor.org/sici?sici=0364-0094%28199223%2917%3A23C165%3ATPORBR%3E2.0.CO%3B2-O.

Kampen, John. *The Hasideans and the Origin of Pharisaism: A Study in 1 and 2 Maccabees*. Septuagint and Cognate Studies 24. Atlanta, GA: Scholars Press, 1988.

Kloppenborg, John S. *Q Parallels: Synopsis, Critical Notes, & Concordance*. Sonoma, CA: Polebridge Press, 1988.

--- *The Shape of Q*. Minneapolis, MN: Augsburg Fortress Press, 1994.

Klutz, Todd E. *Rewriting the* Testament of Solomon: *Tradition, Conflict and Identity in a Late Antique Pseudepigraphon*. London: T&T Clark, 2005. Library of Second Temple Studies 53.

Koester, Helmut. *From Jesus to the Gospels: Interpreting the New Testament in Its Context*. Minneapolis, Fortress Press, 2007.

Lenski, Gerhard. *Power and Privilege: A Theory of Social Stratification*. Chapel Hill and London: University of North Carolina Press, 1984.

Levine, Lee I., ed. *The Galilee in Late Antiquity*. New York and Jerusalem, The Jewish Theological Seminary of America, 1992.

Levine, Lee I. *The Rabbinic Class of Roman Palestine in Late Antiquity*. Jerusalem: The Jewish Theological Seminary of America, 1989.

Loader, William R.G. *Enoch, Levi, and Jubilees on Sexuality: Attitudes towards Sexuality in the Early Enoch Literature, the Aramaic Levi Document, and the Book of Jubilees*. Grand Rapids, MI: Wm. B. Eerdmans Publishing, 2007.

--- *The Pseudepigrapha on Sexuality: Attitudes towards Sexuality in Apocalypses, Testaments, Legends, Wisdom, and Related Literature*. Grand Rapids, MI: Wm. B. Eerdmans Publishing, 2011.

Lövestam, Evald. *Jesus and 'This Generation': A New Testament Study*. Stockholm: Almqvist & Wiksell International, 1995.

MacAdam, Henry Innes. *Geography, Urbanisation and Settlement Patterns in the Roman Near East.* Aldershot GB, Variorum Collected Studies Series, 2002.

MacAdam, Henry Innes. *Studies in the History of the Roman Province of Arabia: The Northern Sector.* BAR International Series, 1986.

Mack, Burton L. *Q: The Lost Sayings Source: Burton Mack's Translation,"* www.tonyburke.ca/wp-content/uploads/Burton-Macks-Q-Text.pdf.

--- *The Lost Gospel: The Book of Q and Christian Origins.* San Francisco: HarperSanFrancisco, 1994.

MacMullen, Ramsey. *Enemies of the Roman Order: Treason, Unrest, and Alienation in the Empire.* London & New York: Routledge, 1996.

Matera, Frank J. *New Testament Theology: Exploring Diversity and Unity.* Louisville, KY., WJKP, 2007.

Metzger, Bruce M. "Letter to the Editor." *Monday Morning: A Magazine for Presbyterian Ministers*, May 15, 1978.

--- "Persistent Problems Confronting Bible Translators," *Bibliotheca Sacra* 150 (July-September 1993).

--- "The Revised Standard Version," *Duke Divinity School Review*, 1979.

Miller, Paul Allen, ed. *Latin Erotic Elegy: An Anthology and Reader.* London & New York: Routledge, 2002.

Murphy, Frederick J. *Early Judaism from the Exile to the Time of Jesus.* Peabody, MA: Hendrickson Publishers, 2002.

Murray, Stephen O. *Homosexualities. Worlds of Desire: The Chicago Series on Sexuality, Gender, and Culture*, University of Chicago Press, 2002.

Neusner, Jacob. *Analysis and Argumentation in Rabbinic Judaism.* Lanham, MD: University Press of America, 2003.

--- *Development of a Legend: Studies on the Traditions Concerning Yoḥanan ben Zakkai.* Netherlands: Brill Academic Publishers, 1970.

--- *First-Century Judaism in Crisis: Yoḥanan ben Zakkai and the Renaissance of Torah.* Nashville: Abingdon Press, 1971.

--- *From Politics to Piety: The Emergence of Pharisaic Judaism.* New York: Ktav Publishing House, 1973.

--- *The Halakhah: An Encyclopaedia of the Law of Judaism.* Leiden: Brill, 2000.

--- *The Idea of Purity in Ancient Judaism: With a Critique and a Commentary by Mary Douglas.* Leiden: Brill Archive, 1973.

--- *A Life of Yoḥanan ben Zakkai (ca. 1-80 C.E.).* Leiden: Brill Archive, 1970.

--- *Rabbinic Literature and the New Testament: What We Cannot Show, We do not Know.* Harrisburg, PA: Trinity Press, 1994.

--- *The Rabbinic Traditions about the Pharisees before 70: The Houses,* Vol. 2. Leiden: Brill Archive, 1971.

Neusner, Jacob and Bruce D. Chilton, eds. *In Quest of the Historical Pharisees.* Waco: Baylor UP, 2007.

Newman, Graeme R. "Sting Operations," Response Guide No. 6, *Center for Problem-Oriented Policing.* http://www.popcenter.org/Responses/sting_operations/1/#endref3, Retrieved 9-18-2018.

Nussbaum, Martha C. and Juha Sihhvola, eds. *The Sleep of Reason: Erotic Experience and Sexual Ethics in Ancient Greece and Rome.* Chicago and London: University of Chicago Press, 2002.

Oakman, Douglas E. *The Political Aims of Jesus.* Minneapolis, MN: Fortress Press, 2012.

Oppenheimer, A'haron. *The 'Am ha-Aretz, A Study in the Social History of the Jewish People in the Hellenistic-Roman Period.* Leiden: Brill, 1977.

Ovid, *Metamorphoses*. Johnson, W.R. Indianapolis, IN: Hackett Publishing, 2010.

Parkhurst, John. *A greek and english Lexicon to the New Testament in which the words and the words and phrases occurring in those sacred books are distinctly explained.* Edinburgh: Thomas Turnbull, 1813.

Pasachoff, Naomi E. and Robert J. Littman. *A Concise History of the Jenowish People.* Lanham, MD: Rowman & Littlefield, 2005.

Petersen, William L., ed. *Gospel Traditions in the Second Century: Origins, Recensions, Text, and Transmission.* Notre Dame and London: University of Notre Dame Press, 1989. Christianity and Judaism in Antiquity. Charles Kannengiesser, series editor. Vol. 3.

Phang, Sara Elise. *The Marriage of Roman Soldiers (13 B.C. – A.D. 235): Law and Family in the Imperial Army.* Brill, 2001. Columbia Studies in the Classical Tradition. Vol XXIV

Piper, Ronald A. *Wisdom in the Q Tradition: The Aphoristic Teaching of Jesus.* Cambridge U.K. and New York: Cambridge UP, 1989. Society for New Testament Studies Monograph Series, General Editor: G.N. Stanton. no. 61.

Polish, David. *Give Us a King: Legal-Religious Sources of Jewish Sovereignty.* Hoboken, NJ: KTAV Publishing, 1989.

Poythress, Vern Sheridan. "Male Meaning in Generic Masculines in Koine Greek." Westminster Theological Journal, 66/2 (2004), 325-36.

Pritz, Ray A. *Nazarene Jewish Christianity: From the End of the New Testament Period until Its Disappearance in the Fourth Century.* Jerusalem & Leiden: The Magnes Press, The Hebrew University. E.J. Brill. 1988. Studia Post-Biblica. Editor J.C.H. Lebram.

Reiling, Jannes L. and J. Swellengrebel, *A Translator's Handbook on the Gospel of Luke.* New York: American Bible Society, 1971.

Rosenblum, Jordan D. "Changing the Subject: Rabbinic Legal Process in the Absence of Justification," *Review of Rabbinic Judaism,* Vol. 18, Issue 1.

Roth, Daniel. *The Story of the 9th of Adar Told through Disagreements.* http://elmad.pardes.org/wp-content/uploads/2014/01/The-Story-of-9Adar-A-Day-of-Disagreement.pdf. Accessed 7/20/2018.

Roth, Jonathan P. *Jewish Military Forces in the Roman Service.* (thesis) San Antonio, TX: San Jose State University, 2004.

Rupp, Leila J. *Sapphistries: A Global History of Love between Women.* NYU Press, 2011.

Saldarini, Anthony J. *Pharisees, Scribes and Sadducees in Palestinian Society: A Sociological Approach.* Grand Rapids, MI and Cambridge: Wm. B. Eerdmans Publishing, 1988.

Schiffman, Lawrence. *Texts and Traditions: A Source Reader for the Study of Second Temple and Rabbinic Judaism.* Jersey City, NJ: KTAV Publishing House, Inc., 1998.

Seland, Torrey. *Establishment Violence in Philo and Luke: A Study of Non-Conformity to the Torah and Jewish Vigilante Reactions.* Leiden; New York; Koln: Brill, 1995.

Shurer, Emil. *The History of the Jewish People in the Age of Jesus Christ (175 B.C.-- A.D. 135)* Revised and Edited by Geza Vermes and Fergus Millar. Edinburgh: T&T Clark, 1973.

Sim, David C. "How Many Jews became Christians in the First Century? The Failure of the Christian Mission to the Jews." HTS 61 (1&2) 2005. (HTS Teologiese Studies/Theological Studies.) https://www.scribd.com/ document/94639523/How-Many-Jews-Became-Christians-in-the-First-Century-the-Failure-of-the-Christian-Mission-to-the-Jews, retrieved 9.9.2015.

Simons, Patricia. *The Sex of Men in Premodern Europe: A Cultural History.* Cambridge, UK; New York: Cambridge UP, 2011.

Stratfor Enterprises, LLC. "Anatomy of a Sting Operation." Apr 16, 2015. https://worldview.stratfor.com/article/anatomy-sting-operation. Retrieved 9-18-2018.

Strickert, Fred. "The Founding of Bethsaida-Julias: Evidence from the Coins of Philip." *Shofar* 13(4), 40-51, 1995.

Thomas, Richard F., ed. *Horace: Odes IV and Carmen Saeculare.* Cambridge UP, 2011.

Topley, Marjorie. *Cantonese Society in Hong Kong and Singapore: Gender, Religion, Medicine and Money; Essays by Marjorie Topley.* Hong Kong, Hong Kong UP, 2011.

Vermès, Géza. *Jesus in the Jewish World.* Norwich, UK: SCM Press, 2010.

Van Voorst, Robert E. *Jesus Outside the New Testament: An Introduction to the Ancient Evidence.* Grand Rapids, MI and Cambridge U.K., Wm. B. Eerdmans Publishing Co., 2000.

Wayman, Richard J. "The Testament of Solomon." (abstract). St. Gimel's College, UK. n.d. http://www.st-Gimels.ac.uk/divinity/rt/otp/guestlectures/harding/

Williams, Gordon. *A Dictionary of Sexual Language and Imagery in Shakespearean and Stuart Literature.* London: Atlantic Highlands, N.J.: Athlone Press, 1994.

Wilson, A.N. *Jesus: A Life.* New York: W.W. Norton, 2004.

Wilson, John Francis. Caesarea Philippi: Banias, the Lost City of Pan. London, L.B. Tauris, 2004. Wiseman, T.P. Classics in Progress: Essays on Ancient Greece and Rome. Oxford UP, 2002.

Youens, Susan. Schubert, Müller, and Die Schöne Müllerin. Cambridge: Cambridge UP, 2006.

Zangenberg, Jürgen, Harold W. Attridge, Dale B. Martin, *Religion, Ethnicity, and Identity in Ancient Galilee: A Region in Transition.* Tübingen: Mohr Siebeck, 2007.

About the Author

RONALD W. GOETZ, recovering fundamentalist, served one year as a C&MA pastor and 13 days in jail for civil disobedience. A former board member of PFLAG and GLSEN, he co-produced the documentary *Holding Families Together*. The self-described "Ecclesiastes Christian" attended two Baptist seminaries, and graduated from San Diego State University and Simpson University. He debunked the Clobber Passage on his blog, biblethumpingliberal.com. Father of two daughters and a gay son, he has four grandchildren. Ron lives with his wife Nital in Southern California.

Made in the USA
Monee, IL
24 January 2020